CLASSROOM DATA TRACKING

Data-Tracking Tools at Your Fingertips!

Grade 3

Carson-Dellosa Publishing, LLC
PO Box 35665
Greensboro, NC 27425 USA
carsondellosa.com

978-1-4838-3441-2
01-158161151

Table of Contents

What Is Classroom Data Tracking?

Being able to prove student growth is more important than ever, making classroom data tracking essential in today's classroom. Data tracking is capturing student learning through both formative and summative assessments and displaying the results. Further assessment of the results can then become an active part of teaching, planning, and remediation. Because teachers are accountable to families and administrators, and time is always at a premium in the classroom, using a simple yet comprehensive data-tracking system is a must.

This book will help make this important data-collection task manageable. The data-tracking tools—charts, rubrics, logs, checklists, inventories, etc.—are easy to use and modifiable to fit any classroom. The tools will help you collect quantitative and qualitative information on each student's level of mastery in any part of your curriculum. Having specific details at your fingertips will aid in setting goals with students, keeping families informed, updating administrators, and displaying progress at student conferences.

An important component of good classroom data tracking is involving students in their own progress so that they can take ownership of their learning. Statistics prove that when students monitor their own learning and track their own growth, they are more highly motivated and perform better. In addition, a good data-tracking system presents avenues for celebrating student successes. Such opportunities are presented here, whether with an "I've done it!" check box or a rating score, and serve to create the intrinsic motivation we all want to see in students.

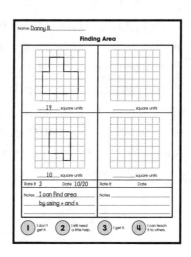 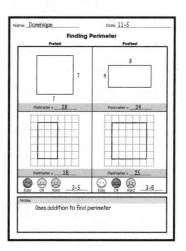

Completed data-tracking sheets for geometric measurement

Why Should I Use Data Tracking?

Teachers are busy and do not need new tasks, but data tracking is a must because in today's data-driven classroom, information is crucial. Fortunately, classroom data tracking can be an at-your-disposal, invaluable tool in many ways:

- Data tracking creates a growth mindset. It shifts focus from a pass/fail mentality to one of showing growth over time.
- It allows you to see any gaps in concepts that need reteaching so that you can easily create focused remediation groups.
- It allows for more targeted lesson planning for the upcoming weeks. Pre-assessments can help you justify spending little to no time on skills that students have already mastered or more time on skills where students lack the expected baseline knowledge. Post-assessments can also help you determine whether students need more time or, if not, what topics you should address next.
- It provides you with daily information and allows you to give students feedback and guidance more regularly.
- It involves students with tracking their own data so that they can easily see their own progress.
- It gives students a sense of pride and ownership over their learning.
- It helps create data portfolios that are useful tools for families, administrators, and student conferences.

Data Tracking in Your Classroom

As standards become more rigorous, data tracking is becoming a necessary part of an already full daily classroom routine. The pages in this book are intended as tools that will help you manage your classroom data and create a customized system to make data tracking more manageable. This book is designed to allow you to choose the reproducibles that work specifically for you and your students. You may even choose to use some reproducibles only for certain groups of students instead of the entire class. This book also allows you to integrate assessments into your current routines by using informal observations and other formative assessments instead of interrupting the flow with traditional tests. If possible, try to involve students in tracking their own data by using reproducibles, graphs, and sample work to create and manage their own portfolios (for more detailed data-tracking management tips, see Managing Data Tracking on pages 8–9).

How to Use This Book

This book includes four main types of pages. Refer to the following sample pages and descriptions to help you get the most out of this resource.

Each anchor and domain section begins with a learning crosswalk. Use the crosswalk to help you better understand what students should know from the previous year and what they will need to know for the next year to better guide your plans for teaching, assessment, and remediation.

A concepts checklist follows the crosswalk for each anchor and domain. Use the checklist to track which concepts you have taught and when. Write the standard code (such as OA.A.1) in the top-left box and describe the concept in the large space. Use some or all of the boxes to the right to list the dates that you taught, tested, and retaught the concept. Make multiple copies as needed.

An explanation page precedes each set of three reproducibles. Use this page to learn about the intended use for each reproducible, to find additional suggestions for use, and to see an example of each reproducible in use.

The type of reproducibles included for each concept will vary according to the types of reproducibles that are most useful for assessing that concept. Reproducibles may include whole-class recording sheets, conference sheets, open-ended assessment pages, or pages where students take charge of their own goals and learning. Use the explanation page before each set to better understand how to use each page.

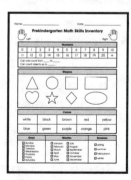

In addition, use the Standards Assessed chart on page 10 to plan for and keep track of the standards and related assessments for a single subject at a glance. Simply record all of the standards for the subject, the dates taught, and any other brief notes you choose to record (assessment types, overall class proficiency, etc.).

Getting Started

You can start data tracking at any point in the school year. If you are new to data tracking, it may be helpful to start small with a single subject until you become more comfortable with the process. Use the following guidelines to help you start a data-tracking system in your classroom (for more detailed data-tracking management tips, see Managing Data Tracking on pages 8–9).

I. Choose the best format for your classroom.
You may choose to have a single binder to collect data or have individual student binders or folders (for more information, see Which Format Is Best? on page 7).

2. Add a cover page.
Because the data-tracking binder will play a starring role in your school year, design an attractive cover that will make the binder identifiable and enjoyable to use. If students are also creating binders or folders, have them add cover pages as well.

3. Organize the binder(s) into sections.
Decide what subjects and topics you will be assessing and use tabs or dividers to clearly divide and label them.

4. Choose a rating system.
Although you may use different systems depending on what and how you will be assessing, use a single rating system for the majority of assessments to create consistency, cohesiveness, and clarity.

Use the following guidelines to help you set a clear tone for the year if using student binders as well.

5. Compose guidelines or a "mission statement."
Guidelines or a short "mission statement" will let students know what is expected of them and make them accountable with their data tracking. If desired, have students keep copies at the beginning of their notebooks and have both students and family members sign them at the beginning of the school year.

6. Have students set long-term and short-term goals.
Long-term goals will give students targets to work toward. Short-term goals will give students attainable checkpoints along the way. It may also be helpful to give students standards checklists in student-friendly language and to have students keep written goals in their binders as reminders.

Other Suggestions

Here are some additional important elements to consider before beginning a data-tracking system:

- *How to recognize students for their successes throughout the year.* Consider ideas such as placing stars programmed with students' names on a Reaching for the Stars bulletin board, giving special rewards, or giving verbal recognition along with a unique class cheer.

- *How to include families in this endeavor.* It can be as simple as sending letters home at the beginning of the year, having student-led conferences using the data binders, or sharing goals with families so that students can work on their goals at home as well.

- *How to maintain student binders.* It may be helpful to provide students with rubrics at the beginning of the year, outlining the expectations for maintaining and assessing their binders periodically to make sure that they continue to include samples and keep the binders neat and organized.

- *How to store student binders.* Decide where to keep the binders—at students' desks or in a separate location. If keeping them in a separate location, you may need to set guidelines for when students can access and add to them.

Which Format Is Best?

Because classroom data-tracking systems need to last for an entire year, many teachers create and maintain them in three-ring binders because of their durability. However, you may choose to keep student work in folders if space is an issue or if students will be storing less information.

A Single Teacher Binder	A Teacher Binder and Student Binders
Pros • Convenient format means the information can always be with you. • You can store all of the information in one place.	**Pros** • Students can move sample work with them each year. • You can include more information because space is not limited. • You have less to do when preparing for conferences.
Cons • You have to gather student work when preparing for conferences. • Space is limited.	**Cons** • It can be time-consuming to work with numerous binders. • It can be challenging to assess class proficiency when sample work is in individual binders.

Managing Data Tracking

Managing the Teacher Binder

- Choose a durable two- or three-inch binder to store all of the important information for the whole year.

- Use the teacher binder as the one place to store the following important assessment-related tools and reproducibles:
  - a copy of the standards at the front of your binder for easy reference
  - copies of the resources and assessment tools for your grade, such as pacing guides, word lists, fluency tests, and reading level charts
  - master copies of assessments (You may also choose to store these separately for space reasons.)

- Consider separating the binder into two sections—overall class proficiency and individual student data. In the class proficiency section, keep information such as what standards you taught when, overall class scores, and student grouping information. Use the individual student section to store running records, baseline tests, remediation forms, and anecdotal notes.

- At the beginning of the school year, assign students numbers and use a set of numbered tabs to organize individual student data in a single place. Add a copy of student names and assigned numbers to the front of the individual data section.

Managing Student Binders

- Consider copying yearlong tracking sheets on card stock instead of copy paper for durability.

- Color code sections to make it easier for students to quickly find the correct pages. For example, copy all sight word pages on yellow paper.

- For younger students, have volunteers preassemble the binders. Include all of the tracking sheets for the year (even if you won't use some until later) to avoid having to add pages later.

- Provide students with several three-hole-punched page protectors for storing sample work, which is often not prepunched.

- Devote a short, designated time each week to allow students to add sample work to and organize their binders.

Tips and Tricks

Organize everything.

- Use file folders to create dividing tabs in a binder. Cut off the half of a file folder with the tab, three-hole punch it, and place it in your binder.
- Keep binders simple by using one pocket for each subject.

Save time.

- Use pens in different colors to make recording dates on a recording sheet simpler. Instead of writing the same date numerous times, simply write the date once in one color and record all of the data from that day using that color. If adding data from another date, repeat with a different color.
- Choose a standard proficiency scale and use it consistently throughout the binder. For example,

E, P, M (emerging, progressing, mastered)	NS, B, OL, A (not seen, beginning, on level, above)
✓–, ✓, ✓+	–, +, ++
a 0–4 rubric	your own unique system

Fit assessment into your day.

- Keep sheets of large labels (such as 2" x 4") on a clipboard. Carry the clipboard throughout the day and use the labels to record any informal observations about individual students. Record each student's name, the date, and your observation on a label. At the end of the day, simply place the label in the corresponding student's section.
- Use your weekly or monthly plan to copy the relevant whole-class progress charts and conference sheets ahead of time. Keep them on a clipboard so that they are at hand when observing students throughout the week or month.
- Focus on assessing or observing only three to five students per day.

Make the reproducibles work for your classroom.

- Add text before copying to create a unique assessment.
- Add, remove, or alter items such as write-on lines or date lines.
- Use a different scale than suggested (see the table above for ideas).
- Use pencil when recording on whole-class checklists so that it is simple to change marks as students progress.
- Use highlighters to draw attention to skills that need remediation, to an individual student's areas of need, or to create targeted small groups.
- Highlight or add stickers beside student goals on graphs and other tracking sheets to give students something visible to work toward.

Standards Assessed

Subject _____   **Quarter** _____

Standard/Topic	Date	Date	Date	Date	Notes

Operations and Algebraic Thinking
Standards Crosswalk

Second Grade

Represent and solve problems involving addition and subtraction.

- Use addition and subtraction within 100 to solve one- and two-step word problems with unknowns in all positions (including those represented by symbols).

Add and subtract within 20.

- Fluently add and subtract within 20 using mental strategies.
- Memorize all sums of two one-digit numbers.

Work with equal groups of objects to gain foundations for multiplication.

- Determine if a group of up to 20 objects represents an odd or even number.
- Use addition to find the total number of objects arranged in rectangular arrays with up to five rows and up to five columns.
- Write an equation to express the sum of an array.

Fourth Grade

Use the four operations with whole numbers to solve problems.

- Interpret a multiplication equation as a comparison.
- Multiply or divide to solve word problems involving multiplicative comparison.
- Solve multistep word problems involving whole numbers using the four operations, including problems in which remainders must be interpreted.
- Represent multistep word problems using equations with a variable.

Gain familiarity with factors and multiples.

- Find all factor pairs for a whole number in the range 1 to 100.
- Understand that a whole number is a multiple of each of its factors.
- Determine whether a given whole number in the range 1 to 100 is prime or composite.

Generate and analyze patterns.

- Generate a number or shape pattern that follows a given rule.

Operations and Algebraic Thinking
Concepts Checklist

Concept		Dates Taught				

Solving Problems Using Multiplication and Division

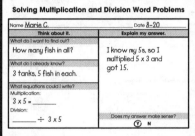

This at-a-glance form is ideal for tracking students' progression in learning to solve problems using multiplication and division. Date the form and record student names in the left-hand column. Mark their levels of achievement by circling *E*, *P*, or *M*. Make copies of this form after you have marked students' names so that you can use it again later.

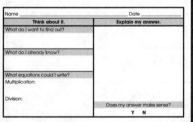

Have students use this form to help them assess their skills in solving word problems. You may print word problems on separate sheets and clip them to this form or print them on a sticky label that you can attach to the back. This will help you make sense of students' notes later.

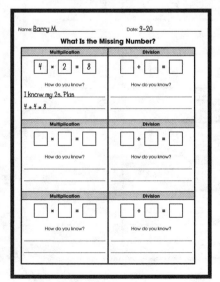

This simple sheet will help you check students' progress as they learn to solve basic multiplication and division problems. Depending on the students' understanding of the two operations, fill in the first two boxes and allow them to answer it; or leave any one box blank to allow students to find the missing number. Beyond their ease with the mechanics of the problem, especially note their reasoning skills.

Using Multiplication and Division

E = Emerging P = Progressing M = Mastery Date **Students**	Interpret products	Interpret quotients	Solve word problems	Determine unknown numbers	Use strategies
	E P M	E P M	E P M	E P M	E P M
	E P M	E P M	E P M	E P M	E P M
	E P M	E P M	E P M	E P M	E P M
	E P M	E P M	E P M	E P M	E P M
	E P M	E P M	E P M	E P M	E P M
	E P M	E P M	E P M	E P M	E P M
	E P M	E P M	E P M	E P M	E P M
	E P M	E P M	E P M	E P M	E P M
	E P M	E P M	E P M	E P M	E P M
	E P M	E P M	E P M	E P M	E P M
	E P M	E P M	E P M	E P M	E P M
	E P M	E P M	E P M	E P M	E P M
	E P M	E P M	E P M	E P M	E P M
	E P M	E P M	E P M	E P M	E P M
	E P M	E P M	E P M	E P M	E P M
	E P M	E P M	E P M	E P M	E P M
	E P M	E P M	E P M	E P M	E P M
	E P M	E P M	E P M	E P M	E P M
	E P M	E P M	E P M	E P M	E P M
	E P M	E P M	E P M	E P M	E P M

Solving Multiplication and Division Word Problems

Name _____ Date _____

Think about it.	Explain my answer.
What do I want to find out?	
What do I already know?	
What equations could I write? Multiplication: Division:	**Does my answer make sense?** Y N

Name _____ Date _____

Think about it.	Explain my answer.
What do I want to find out?	
What do I already know?	
What equations could I write? Multiplication: Division:	**Does my answer make sense?** Y N

What Is the Missing Number?

Multiplication	Division
☐ × ☐ = ☐	☐ ÷ ☐ = ☐
How do you know?	How do you know?
_____	_____
_____	_____

Multiplication	Division
☐ × ☐ = ☐	☐ ÷ ☐ = ☐
How do you know?	How do you know?
_____	_____
_____	_____

Multiplication	Division
☐ × ☐ = ☐	☐ ÷ ☐ = ☐
How do you know?	How do you know?
_____	_____
_____	_____

Multiplication and Division Fluency

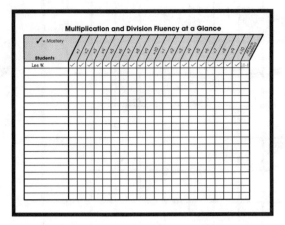

This form will allow you to see at a glance which multiplication and division facts students have mastered. Record student names in the left-hand column. Give students sheets of paper with written multiplication or division facts for one set of facts (2s, 5s, etc.) without answers. Slip the sheets into sheet protectors and give students write-on/wipe-off markers. Students should to be able to answer one set of facts in less than a minute. Place check marks in the appropriate columns based on student mastery.

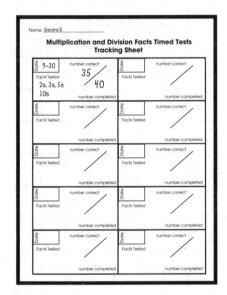

Use this simple sheet to track a student's progress over time. After giving the student a timed test, simply record the date, the facts you tested, and the number correct of the total presented. Test these facts orally or with a write-on/wipe-off sheet as described above.

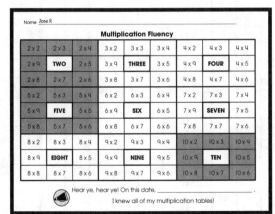

Challenge students to show what they know of their multiplication tables. This could be accomplished as a student-teacher activity or peer pairing. You or a peer will read the facts surrounding any number word. Students will then color or circle the facts that they know. Have students mark any problem facts for extra practice. Finally, students can mark the date they mastered all multiplication facts.

Multiplication and Division Fluency at a Glance

Students	✓ = Mastery	×1	×2	×3	×4	×5	×6	×7	×8	×9	×10	÷1	÷2	÷3	÷4	÷5	÷6	÷7	÷8	÷9	÷10	All facts mastered

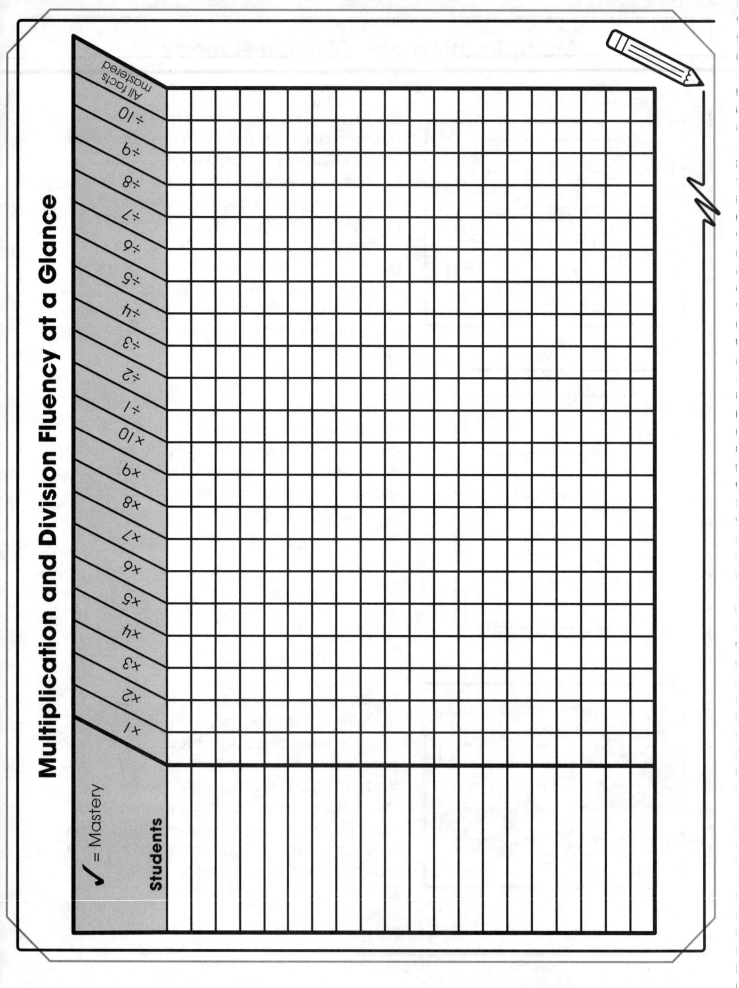

Name: _____

Multiplication and Division Facts Timed Tests
Tracking Sheet

Date	number correct
Facts Tested	
	number completed

Date	number correct
Facts Tested	
	number completed

Date	number correct
Facts Tested	
	number completed

Date	number correct
Facts Tested	
	number completed

Date	number correct
Facts Tested	
	number completed

Date	number correct
Facts Tested	
	number completed

Date	number correct
Facts Tested	
	number completed

Date	number correct
Facts Tested	
	number completed

Date	number correct
Facts Tested	
	number completed

Date	number correct
Facts Tested	
	number completed

Multiplication Fluency

Name: _____

2 x 2	2 x 3	2 x 4		3 x 2	3 x 3	3 x 4	4 x 2	4 x 3	4 x 4
2 x 9	**TWO**	2 x 5		3 x 9	**THREE**	3 x 5	4 x 9	**FOUR**	4 x 5
2 x 8	2 x 7	2 x 6		3 x 8	3 x 7	3 x 6	4 x 8	4 x 7	4 x 6
5 x 2	5 x 3	5 x 4		6 x 2	6 x 3	6 x 4	7 x 2	7 x 3	7 x 4
5 x 9	**FIVE**	5 x 5		6 x 9	**SIX**	6 x 5	7 x 9	**SEVEN**	7 x 5
5 x 8	5 x 7	5 x 6		6 x 8	6 x 7	6 x 6	7 x 8	7 x 7	7 x 6
8 x 2	8 x 3	8 x 4		9 x 2	9 x 3	9 x 4	10 x 2	10 x 3	10 x 4
8 x 9	**EIGHT**	8 x 5		9 x 9	**NINE**	9 x 5	10 x 9	**TEN**	10 x 5
8 x 8	8 x 7	8 x 6		9 x 8	9 x 7	9 x 6	10 x 8	10 x 7	10 x 6

Hear ye, hear ye! On this date, _____

I knew all of my multiplication tables!

Number and Operations in Base Ten
Standards Crosswalk

Second Grade

Understand place value.

- Understand that the digits of a three-digit number represent amounts of hundreds, tens, and ones.
- Think of 100 as a bundle of 10 tens or a "hundred".
- Understand that the multiples of 100 (through 900) refer to 1 to 9 hundreds, 0 tens, and 0 ones.
- Count within 1,000.
- Skip-count by 5s, 10s, and 100s.
- Read and write numbers to 1,000 using numerals, number names, and expanded form.
- Use >, =, and < to compare two three-digit numbers.

Use place value understanding and properties of operations to add and subtract.

- Fluently add and subtract within 100.
- Add up to four two-digit numbers.
- Add and subtract within 1,000, relating the strategies used to a written method.
- Mentally add or subtract 10 or 100 to or from a given number 100 to 900.
- Explain why addition and subtraction strategies work.

Fourth Grade

Generalize place value understanding for multi-digit whole numbers.

- Recognize that each place value is 10 times greater than the one to its right.
- Read and write multi-digit whole numbers using numerals, words, or expanded form.
- Compare two multi-digit numbers using >, =, and <.
- Round multi-digit whole numbers to any place.

Use place value understanding and properties of operations to perform multi-digit arithmetic.

- Fluently add and subtract multi-digit whole numbers.
- Multiply whole numbers of up to four digits by a one-digit number and two two-digit numbers.
- Find whole-number quotients and remainders with up to four-digit dividends and one-digit divisors.

Number and Operations in Base Ten
Concepts Checklist

Concept		Dates Taught				

Place Value

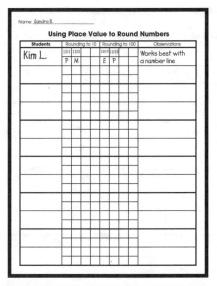

This form will allow you to see at a glance which students have mastered the concepts of rounding to tens and hundreds and which need extra help. First, record student names in the left-hand column. Take note of progress as the unit is introduced, practiced, and concluded with whatever scale you prefer, such as *E* (Emerging), *P* (Progressing), and *M* (Mastery). Write notes about students' successes and challenges in the *Observations* section.

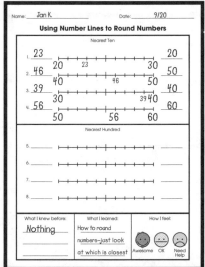

Allow students to show what they understand about two- and three-digit place value by rounding whole numbers to the nearest ten or hundred. Write numbers for students to round in the spaces at the left. Have students mark the number line to calculate or check their answers. When this page is complete, have students fill in what they knew before and what they have learned. Finally, have students rate themselves by coloring or circling the appropriate face.

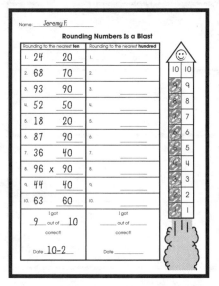

Use this sheet to record students' abilities in rounding numbers to the nearest ten or the nearest hundred. Use the sheet on two different dates—first while students round to the nearest ten and second while students round to the nearest hundred. Have students mark how many they had correct out of the number tried. Add the date. Have students rate themselves by coloring the correct number of squares on the rocket. If students like, have them draw a face in the front end of the rocket to show their feelings.

Using Place Value to Round Numbers

Students	Rounding to 10				Rounding to 100				Observations

Name: _____ Date: _____

Using Number Lines to Round Numbers

Nearest Ten

1. _____ |—+—+—+—+—+—|—+—+—+—+—| _____

2. _____ |—+—+—+—+—+—|—+—+—+—+—| _____

3. _____ |—+—+—+—+—+—|—+—+—+—+—| _____

4. _____ |—+—+—+—+—+—|—+—+—+—+—| _____

Nearest Hundred

5. _____ |—+—+—+—+—+—|—+—+—+—+—| _____

6. _____ |—+—+—+—+—+—|—+—+—+—+—| _____

7. _____ |—+—+—+—+—+—|—+—+—+—+—| _____

8. _____ |—+—+—+—+—+—|—+—+—+—+—| _____

What I knew before:	What I learned:	How I feel:
_____	_____	
_____	_____	Awesome OK Need Help
_____	_____	

Name: _____

Rounding Numbers Is a Blast!

Rounding to the nearest **ten**	Rounding to the nearest **hundred**
1. _____	1. _____
2. _____	2. _____
3. _____	3. _____
4. _____	4. _____
5. _____	5. _____
6. _____	6. _____
7. _____	7. _____
8. _____	8. _____
9. _____	9. _____
10. _____	10. _____
I got _____ out of _____ correct!	I got _____ out of _____ correct!
Date _____	Date _____

Multi-Digit Arithmetic

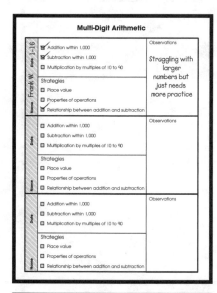

Attach copies of this conference sheet to a clipboard for easy note taking during spot observations while students work with fractions and decimals. Record the student's name and date, and check off the appropriate boxes based on your observation. Use the *Observations* section to record any successes or recommendations.

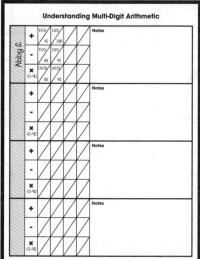

Use this easy-to-use sheet to test multi-digit arithmetic skills over a period of time or for pretesting and posttesting. Record a student's name in the left-hand column. Then, record the date and score as you assess any of the operations listed. Use the *Notes* section to record any observations, strategies, or recommendations.

Use this form for assessing addition, subtraction, and multiplication concepts. Have students record the date in each of the top-left boxes if assessing over time. If assessing on a single date, have students use just the top-left box to record the date. Provide students with a problem and have them copy and solve it in the large blank space. Then, have students use the 1-4 scale at the bottom to self-assess their work.

Multi-Digit Arithmetic

Date		Observations
	☐ Addition within 1,000	
	☐ Subtraction within 1,000	
	☐ Multiplication by multiples of 10 to 90	

Strategies

☐ Place value

☐ Properties of operations

☐ Relationship between addition and subtraction

Date		Observations
	☐ Addition within 1,000	
	☐ Subtraction within 1,000	
	☐ Multiplication by multiples of 10 to 90	

Strategies

☐ Place value

☐ Properties of operations

☐ Relationship between addition and subtraction

Date		Observations
	☐ Addition within 1,000	
	☐ Subtraction within 1,000	
	☐ Multiplication by multiples of 10 to 90	

Strategies

☐ Place value

☐ Properties of operations

☐ Relationship between addition and subtraction

Name

Understanding Multi-Digit Arithmetic

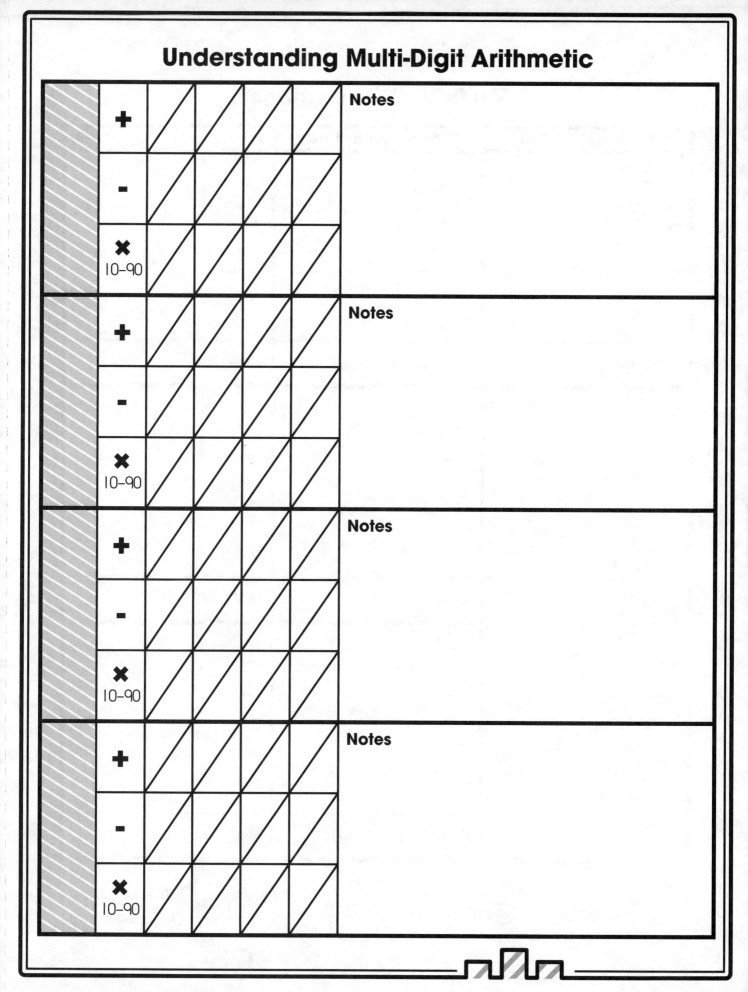

+

-

✖
10–90

Notes

+

-

✖
10–90

Notes

+

-

✖
10–90

Notes

+

-

✖
10–90

Notes

Multi-Digit Operations

Addition to 1,000	Subtraction to 1,000	Multiplication by 10–90
Rate It	**Rate It**	**Rate It**
Rate It	**Rate It**	**Rate It**
Rate It	**Rate It**	**Rate It**

 I don't understand yet.

 I can solve problems with help.

 I can solve problems correctly.

 I can teach it to others.

Number and Operations—Fractions
Standards Crosswalk

Second Grade

*The Number and Operations—Fractions domain begins in third grade.
Geometry

Reason with shapes and their attributes.

- Partition a rectangle into rows and columns of same-size squares and count to find the total number of them.
- Partition circles and rectangles into two, three, or four equal shares, using the words *halves, thirds, half of, a fourth of,* etc., to describe them.
- Describe a divided whole as two halves, three thirds, or four fourths.
- Recognize that equal shares of identical wholes may not have the same shape.

Fourth Grade

Extend understanding of fraction equivalence and ordering.

- Recognize and form equivalent fractions.
- Compare two fractions with different numerators and different denominators using >, =, and <.

Build fractions from unit fractions by applying and extending previous understandings of operations on whole numbers.

- Understand fractions with numerators greater than one as sums of unit fractions 1/b.
- Add and subtract mixed numbers with like denominators.
- Multiply a fraction by a whole number.
- Understand fractions with numerators greater than one as multiples of the unit fraction 1/b.

Understand decimal notation for fractions and compare decimal fractions.

- Rename and add fractions with denominators of 10 and 100.
- Rewrite fractions with denominators of 10 or 100 as decimals.

Number and Operations—Fractions
Concepts Checklist

Concept		Dates Taught				

Understanding Fractions

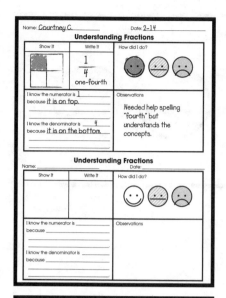

Use this conference sheet for one-on-one follow-ups after introducing fractions to students. After you name a fraction, have students show a model of the fraction and then write its name. Have them tell what they know about numerators and denominators by completing the two statements on the left. Finally, have students rate themselves by coloring or circling the appropriate face.

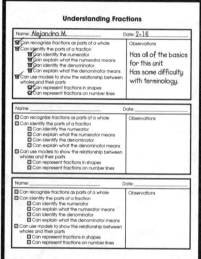

Use this page to track students' proficiencies with each skill involved in understanding fractions. Record the student's name and date in the top box. As a student demonstrates proficiency with any skill, check the box. Use the *Observations* section to record more detailed information or recommendations.

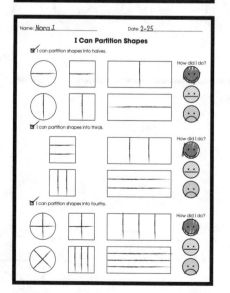

Use this page to help students show their knowledge of partitioning shapes into halves, thirds, and fourths. Ask students to partition each shape in two different ways. As they complete a section successfully, have students check the "I can" box on the left and rate the level of difficulty on the right.

Name: _____ Date: _____

Understanding Fractions

Show It	Write It

How did I do?

I know the numerator is _____

because _____

_____

_____.

I know the denominator is _____

because _____

_____

_____.

Observations

Name: _____ Date: _____

Understanding Fractions

Show It	Write It

How did I do?

I know the numerator is _____

because _____

_____

_____.

I know the denominator is _____

because _____

_____

_____.

Observations

Understanding Fractions

Name: _____ **Date:** _____

	Observations

☐ Can recognize fractions as parts of a whole
☐ Can identify the parts of a fraction
    ☐ Can identify the numerator
    ☐ Can explain what the numerator means
    ☐ Can identify the denominator
    ☐ Can explain what the denominator means
☐ Can use models to show the relationship between wholes and their parts
    ☐ Can represent fractions in shapes
    ☐ Can represent fractions on number lines	

Name: _____ **Date:** _____

	Observations

☐ Can recognize fractions as parts of a whole
☐ Can identify the parts of a fraction
    ☐ Can identify the numerator
    ☐ Can explain what the numerator means
    ☐ Can identify the denominator
    ☐ Can explain what the denominator means
☐ Can use models to show the relationship between wholes and their parts
    ☐ Can represent fractions in shapes
    ☐ Can represent fractions on number lines	

Name: _____ **Date:** _____

	Observations

☐ Can recognize fractions as parts of a whole
☐ Can identify the parts of a fraction
    ☐ Can identify the numerator
    ☐ Can explain what the numerator means
    ☐ Can identify the denominator
    ☐ Can explain what the denominator means
☐ Can use models to show the relationship between wholes and their parts
    ☐ Can represent fractions in shapes
    ☐ Can represent fractions on number lines	

I Can Partition Shapes

☐ I can partition shapes into halves.

How did I do?

☐ I can partition shapes into thirds.

How did I do?

☐ I can partition shapes into fourths.

How did I do?

Representing Fractions

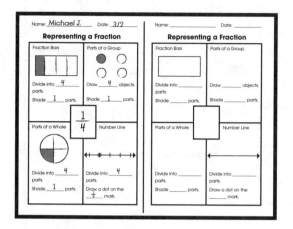

This sheet will show what students understand about representing fractions. Write a fraction in the center box. Then, have students represent the fraction in various ways by filling in the blanks, drawing and shading figures, and marking the number line. Each representation must match the center fraction.

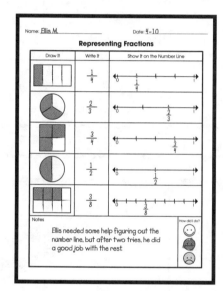

This sheet asks students to represent fractions in three different ways. For each section, give students a fraction orally. In the *Draw It* section, have students draw models, then divide and shade them to match the fraction given. In the *Write It* section, have students write the fraction in numerals or words. Finally, have students divide the number line appropriately and write the fraction where it belongs. Use the *Notes* section to record observations, strategies, or recommendations. Finally, have students rate themselves by coloring or circling the appropriate face.

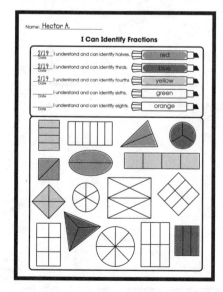

Students can use this page to track their learning during a unit on identifying fractions. The page is simple and fun. Have students read each sentence and color the matching models with the color written on the marker. If their work is correct, they should write the date in front of the appropriate sentence. Students may be able to complete the entire page at once. If not, you will be able to follow up based on those sentences not dated.

Name: _____   Date: _____

Representing a Fraction

Fraction Bars	Parts of a Group
[rectangle]	Draw _____ objects.
Divide into _____ parts.	Shade _____ parts.
Shade _____ parts.	

Parts of a Whole	Number Line
Divide into _____ parts.	Divide into _____ parts.
Shade _____ parts.	Draw a dot on the _____ mark.

Name: _____   Date: _____

Representing a Fraction

Fraction Bars	Parts of a Group
[rectangle]	Draw _____ objects.
Divide into _____ parts.	Shade _____ parts.
Shade _____ parts.	

Parts of a Whole	Number Line
Divide into _____ parts.	Divide into _____ parts.
Shade _____ parts.	Draw a dot on the _____ mark.

Representing Fractions

Draw It	Write It	Show It on the Number Line
	——	0 ——————————————— 1
	——	0 ——————————————— 1
	——	0 ——————————————— 1
	——	0 ——————————————— 1
	——	0 ——————————————— 1

Notes

How did I do?

I Can Identify Fractions

_____ I understand and can identify halves.
Date

_____ I understand and can identify thirds.
Date

_____ I understand and can identify fourths
Date

_____ I understand and can identify sixths.
Date

_____ I understand and can identify eights.
Date

red

blue

yellow

green

orange

Name: _____

40

Equivalent Fractions

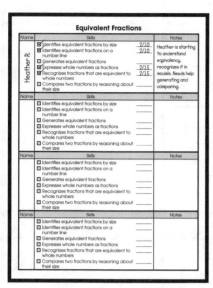

Use this page to track students' proficiency with each skill involved with understanding equivalent fractions. Record each student's name in the left-hand column. As each student demonstrates proficiency with a skill, check the box and record the date. Use the *Notes* section to record more detailed information and observations.

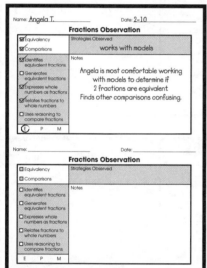

Use this page to record more detailed information about a formal or informal assessment. As you observe a student working with fractions, place a check mark beside observed skills. Record any strategies observed and use the *Notes* section to record any additional observations. Then, circle *E*, *P*, or *M* to show if the skills observed are emerging, progressing, or mastered. Store a copy of the student's work with the assessment.

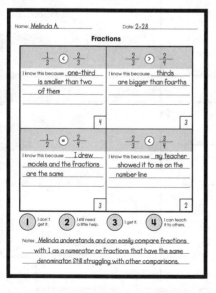

Use this sheet to test how well students are able to compare fractions. Have they developed good fraction sense? Write the fractions in each box or dictate them. Students will then place a comparative symbol in the circle. They should explain their choice on the lines below. Then, have students use the 1–4 scale at the bottom to self-assess each problem. Finally, use the *Notes* section to record any observations, strategies, or recommendations.

Equivalent Fractions

Name	Skills	Notes
	☐ Identifies equivalent fractions by size _____	
	☐ Identifies equivalent fractions on a number line _____	
	☐ Generates equivalent fractions _____	
	☐ Expresses whole numbers as fractions _____	
	☐ Recognizes fractions that are equivalent to whole numbers _____	
	☐ Compares two fractions by reasoning about their size _____	

Name	Skills	Notes
	☐ Identifies equivalent fractions by size _____	
	☐ Identifies equivalent fractions on a number line _____	
	☐ Generates equivalent fractions _____	
	☐ Expresses whole numbers as fractions _____	
	☐ Recognizes fractions that are equivalent to whole numbers _____	
	☐ Compares two fractions by reasoning about their size _____	

Name	Skills	Notes
	☐ Identifies equivalent fractions by size _____	
	☐ Identifies equivalent fractions on a number line _____	
	☐ Generates equivalent fractions _____	
	☐ Expresses whole numbers as fractions _____	
	☐ Recognizes fractions that are equivalent to whole numbers _____	
	☐ Compares two fractions by reasoning about their size _____	

Name	Skills	Notes
	☐ Identifies equivalent fractions by size _____	
	☐ Identifies equivalent fractions on a number line _____	
	☐ Generates equivalent fractions _____	
	☐ Expresses whole numbers as fractions _____	
	☐ Recognizes fractions that are equivalent to whole numbers _____	
	☐ Compares two fractions by reasoning about their size _____	

Name: _____ Date: _____

Fractions Observation

	Strategies Observed
☐ Equivalency ☐ Comparisons	
☐ Identifies equivalent fractions ☐ Generates equivalent fractions ☐ Expresses whole numbers as fractions ☐ Relates fractions to whole numbers ☐ Uses reasoning to compare fractions	Notes
E P M	

Name: _____ Date: _____

Fractions Observation

	Strategies Observed
☐ Equivalency ☐ Comparisons	
☐ Identifies equivalent fractions ☐ Generates equivalent fractions ☐ Expresses whole numbers as fractions ☐ Relates fractions to whole numbers ☐ Uses reasoning to compare fractions	Notes
E P M	

Fractions

___ ___ ◯ ___ ___

I know this because _____

_____

_____

_____ .

___ ___ ◯ ___ ___

I know this because _____

_____

_____

_____ .

___ ___ ◯ ___ ___

I know this because _____

_____

_____

_____ .

___ ___ ◯ ___ ___

I know this because _____

_____

_____

_____ .

1 I don't get it.   **2** I still need a little help.   **3** I get it.   **4** I can teach it to others.

Notes _____

_____

_____

Measurement and Data Standards Crosswalk

Second Grade

Measure and estimate lengths in standard units.

- Measure the length of an object by selecting and using appropriate tools.
- Measure the length of an object using two different length units and relate the measurements to the units used.
- Estimate lengths using units of inches, feet, centimeters, and meters.
- Measure to determine how much longer one object is than another.

Relate addition and subtraction to length.

- Use addition and subtraction within 100 to solve word problems involving lengths given in the same units.
- Represent whole numbers as lengths from 0 on a number line and represent whole-number sums and differences within 100 on a number line.

Work with time and money.

- Tell and write time from analog and digital clocks to the nearest five minutes, using am and pm.
- Solve word problems involving dollar bills, quarters, dimes, nickels, and pennies, using $ and ¢ symbols appropriately.

Represent and interpret data.

- Measure objects and represent measurements on a line plot (nearest whole unit).
- Draw picture and bar graphs (with single-unit scales) for four categories.
- Solve simple addition, subtraction, and comparison problems using information given in a graph.

Fourth Grade

Solve problems involving measurement and conversion of measurements from a larger unit to a smaller unit.

- Know relative sizes of measurement units within one system of units including km, m, cm; kg, g; lb., oz.; l, mL; hr., min., sec.
- Convert measurements within a measurement system.
- Use the four operations to solve measurement word problems.
- Use the area and perimeter formulas for rectangles.

Represent and interpret data.

- Create line plots displaying fractions (1/2, 1/4, 1/8).
- Solve problems involving addition and subtraction of data from line plots.

Geometric measurement: understand concepts of angle and measure angles.

- Recognize that angles are formed by two rays with the same endpoint.
- Understand that an angle is measured in degrees of a circle.
- Measure and draw whole-number angles using a protractor.
- Understand that the sum of an angle's parts is equal to the whole angle.
- Solve addition and subtraction problems to find unknown angles.

Measurement and Data Concepts Checklist

Concept		Dates Taught				

Time Concepts

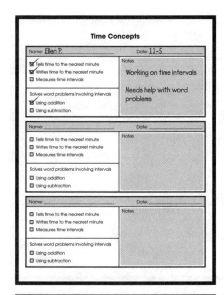

Attach copies of this observation sheet to a clipboard for easy note taking during spot observations while students work on time concepts. Record each student's name and date, and check off which time concepts you are observing. Be sure to note strengths, recommendations, and specific observations.

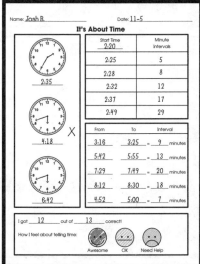

This sheet will allow students to show what they know about elapsed time. Before handing out the sheet, fill in some of the spaces and reproduce it. Write three times of day under the clocks on the left. Have students draw hands to match. On the left, write a start time and various minute intervals on the right side of the top section. Have students write the time that matches each interval given. In the bottom section, fill in the *From* and *To* boxes so that students can find the intervals between each pair of times. Finally, have students rate themselves by writing the number they got correct out of the total and by coloring or circling the appropriate face.

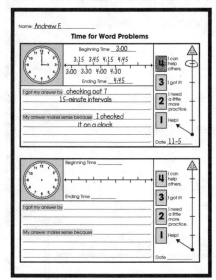

This form will allow students to show what they know about time intervals. Ask students to find an answer to a word problem you have given them by showing the lapse of time on a number line. Have students decide on appropriate intervals and label the number line. Then, have them complete the two sentences. Finally, have them rate their understanding and mark it on the "big hand."

Time Concepts

Name:_____ Date:_____

☐ Tells time to the nearest minute

☐ Writes time to the nearest minute

☐ Measures time intervals

Solves word problems involving intervals

☐ Using addition

☐ Using subtraction

Notes

Name:_____ Date:_____

☐ Tells time to the nearest minute

☐ Writes time to the nearest minute

☐ Measures time intervals

Solves word problems involving intervals

☐ Using addition

☐ Using subtraction

Notes

Name:_____ Date:_____

☐ Tells time to the nearest minute

☐ Writes time to the nearest minute

☐ Measures time intervals

Solves word problems involving intervals

☐ Using addition

☐ Using subtraction

Notes

It's About Time

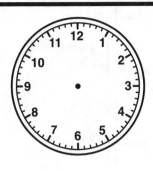

_____

_____

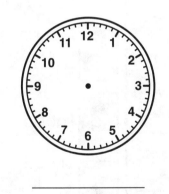

_____

Start Time _____	Minute Intervals

From	To	Interval
_____	_____ = _____ minutes
_____	_____ = _____ minutes
_____	_____ = _____ minutes
_____	_____ = _____ minutes
_____	_____ = _____ minutes

I got _____ out of _____ correct!

How I feel about telling time:

Awesome

OK

Need Help

Time for Word Problems

Beginning Time _____

Ending Time _____

I got my answer by _____
_____
_____.

My answer makes sense because _____
_____
_____
_____.

4 I can help others.

3 I got it!

2 I need a little more practice.

1 Help!

Date _____

Beginning Time _____

Ending Time _____

I got my answer by _____
_____
_____.

My answer makes sense because _____
_____
_____
_____.

4 I can help others.

3 I got it!

2 I need a little more practice.

1 Help!

Date _____

Measuring and Estimating Volume and Mass

Use this page to record your class's recognition and understanding of essential measurement terms at this level. Using either formal or informal assessments and a scale of your choosing (or the *E*, *P*, and *M* scale shown here), record individual student proficiencies for each vocabulary term.

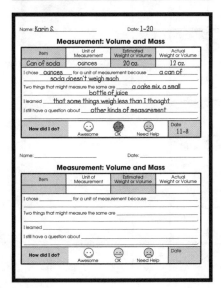

Attach copies of this conference sheet to a clipboard for easy note taking during spot observations while students solve word problems. Record each student's name and date and check off the appropriate boxes based on your observation. Use the **Observations** section to record any successes or recommendations.

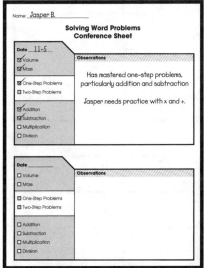

This form will allow students to show how much measurement sense they have. Have students choose an item to weigh, determine the unit of measurement to use, estimate the item's weight, and then weigh it and compare the actual weight with the estimation. Then, have students explain and expand their thinking by completing the sentences. Finally, have students rate themselves by coloring or circling the appropriate face and dating the form.

Measurement Terms

E = Emerging P = Progressing M = Mastery Students	solid	liquid	mass	volume	capacity	weight	estimate	gram	kilogram	liter	Notes

Name: _____

Solving Word Problems Conference Sheet

Date _____

☐ Volume
☐ Mass

☐ One-Step Problems
☐ Two-Step Problems

☐ Addition
☐ Subtraction
☐ Multiplication
☐ Division

Observations

Date _____

☐ Volume
☐ Mass

☐ One-Step Problems
☐ Two-Step Problems

☐ Addition
☐ Subtraction
☐ Multiplication
☐ Division

Observations

Name: _____   Date: _____

Measurement: Volume and Mass

Item	Unit of Measurement	Estimated Weight or Volume	Actual Weight or Volume

I chose _____ for a unit of measurement because _____
_____.

Two things that might measure the same are _____
_____.

I learned _____.

I still have a question about _____
_____.

How did I do?	:) Awesome	:| OK	:(Need Help	Date

Name: _____   Date: _____

Measurement: Volume and Mass

Item	Unit of Measurement	Estimated Weight or Volume	Actual Weight or Volume

I chose _____ for a unit of measurement because _____
_____.

Two things that might measure the same are _____
_____.

I learned _____.

I still have a question about _____
_____.

How did I do?	:) Awesome	:| OK	:(Need Help	Date

Representing Data

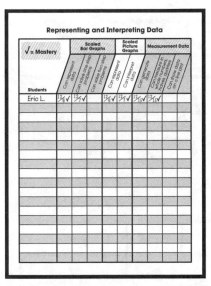

Third-grade students need to be able to work with scaled bar graphs, scaled picture graphs, and line plots. As a student demonstrates proficiency with a skill marked, write the date and make a check mark to show mastery. This form will allow you to see at a glance which students have mastered the skills and which need extra help.

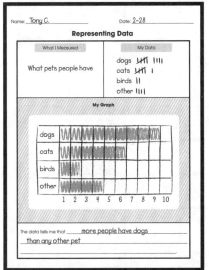

Use this form to assess whether students are able to make their own bar or picture graphs. First, have students choose a topic to gather data on and write it in the top left section. Have them record their data in the top right section. The middle section allows them to draw either a bar or picture graph for recording their data. In the last section, have students write the conclusion they drew from looking at their data.

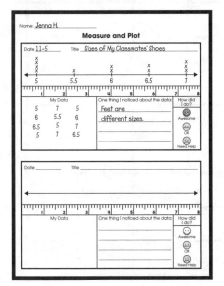

Use this form to assess whether students are able to show their data correctly on a line plot. After dating the form at the top left, students should choose and write a title. Have them record their data in the bottom-left section and then plot it on the number line above. The data should show them something, which they will record in the middle section. Finally, have students rate how they think they did by coloring or circling the appropriate face.

Representing and Interpreting Data

√ = Mastery	Scaled Bar Graphs			Scaled Picture Graphs		Measurement Data		
Students	Can represent data	Can solve one-step problems	Can solve two-step problems	Can represent data	Can interpret data	Can generate data	Can measure in whole numbers, halves, quarters	Can show data on a line plot

Representing Data

What I Measured	My Data

My Graph

The data tells me that _____

_____

_____

Name: _____

Measure and Plot

Date _____   Title _____

My Data	One thing I noticed about the data:	How did I do?
	_____ _____ _____ _____	☺ Awesome ☺ OK ☹ Need Help

Date _____   Title _____

My Data	One thing I noticed about the data:	How did I do?
	_____ _____ _____ _____	☺ Awesome ☺ OK ☹ Need Help

Geometric Measurement

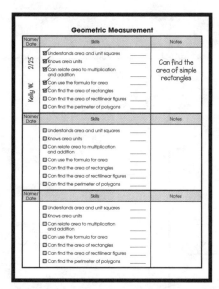

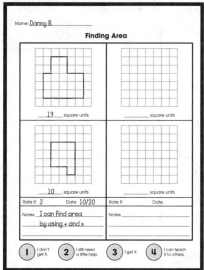

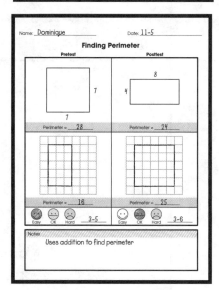

Attach copies of this conference sheet to a clipboard for easy note taking during spot observations while students work on geometric measurement. Record each student's name and date, and check off the appropriate boxes based on your observation. Use the *Notes* section to record any successes or recommendations.

This sheet will allow students to show what they know about finding area. If handing these out to a group or the entire class, outline a shape in each grid before reproducing the form for the class. Have students show what they know by writing the total number of square units shown in each grid. Have students use the 1–4 scale at the bottom to self-assess their work on each problem. The sheet includes two *Notes* sections for students to complete if you present items on two different dates.

Use this form to measure how well students understand the concept of perimeter. The form is intended for use as a pretest and posttest. In the top boxes, give students the measurement of two sides, either orally or on the board. Have students figure out the perimeter of each. In the bottom boxes, have students draw a figure of any size and write the perimeters. Depending on the students, you may want to give them the perimeters and have them write the sides of the figure or draw the figure on the grid.

Geometric Measurement

Name/Date	Skills	Notes
	☐ Understands area and unit squares _____	
	☐ Knows area units _____	
	☐ Can relate area to multiplication and addition _____	
	☐ Can use the formula for area _____	
	☐ Can find the area of rectangles _____	
	☐ Can find the area of rectilinear figures _____	
	☐ Can find the perimeter of polygons _____	
Name/Date	Skills	Notes
	☐ Understands area and unit squares _____	
	☐ Knows area units _____	
	☐ Can relate area to multiplication and addition _____	
	☐ Can use the formula for area _____	
	☐ Can find the area of rectangles _____	
	☐ Can find the area of rectilinear figures _____	
	☐ Can find the perimeter of polygons _____	
Name/Date	Skills	Notes
	☐ Understands area and unit squares _____	
	☐ Knows area units _____	
	☐ Can relate area to multiplication and addition _____	
	☐ Can use the formula for area _____	
	☐ Can find the area of rectangles _____	
	☐ Can find the area of rectilinear figures _____	
	☐ Can find the perimeter of polygons _____	

Finding Area

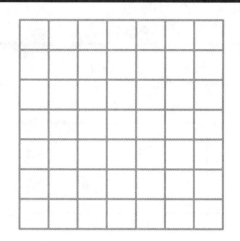

_____ square units

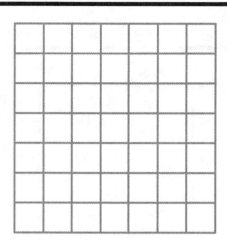

_____ square units

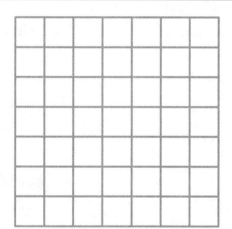

_____ square units

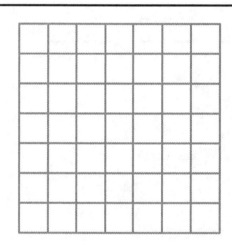

_____ square units

Rate It	Date	Rate It	Date

Notes _____

_____

_____

Notes _____

_____

_____

 I don't get it.   I still need a little help.   I get it.   I can teach it to others.

Finding Perimeter

Pretest	**Posttest**

Perimeter = _____

Perimeter = _____

Perimeter = _____

Perimeter = _____

☺ Easy   ☺ OK   ☹ Hard   _____

☺ Easy   ☺ OK   ☹ Hard   _____

Notes

Geometry Standards Crosswalk

Second Grade

Reason with shapes and their attributes.

- Recognize and draw shapes with specific attributes.
- Identify triangles, quadrilaterals, pentagons, hexagons, and cubes.
- Partition a rectangle into rows and columns of same-size squares and count to find the total number of them.
- Partition circles and rectangles into two, three, or four equal shares, using the words *halves, thirds, half of, a fourth of,* etc., to describe them.
- Describe a divided whole as two halves, three thirds, or four fourths.
- Recognize that equal shares of identical wholes may not have the same shape.

Fourth Grade

Draw and identify lines and angles, and classify shapes by properties of their lines and angles.

- Draw and identify points, lines, line segments, rays, angles, and perpendicular and parallel lines in two-dimensional figures.
- Classify polygons by the types of angles and lines used to form them.
- Recognize that lines of symmetry divide a shape into matching parts.
- Identify symmetrical shapes.
- Draw lines of symmetry.

Geometry Concepts Checklist

Concept		Dates Taught			

Identifying Shapes

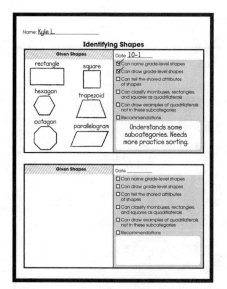

This form is perfect for tracking whether students can name, draw, and classify third-grade-level shapes. Present pictures or drawings of the shapes and name them in the left section. Elicit answers about the name and attributes of each. Then, ask students to draw a shape in the box when you name it. Finally, have students sort the shape pictures or drawings and give reasons for the sort. As you observe their work, check off the appropriate boxes in the right section. Record any recommendations you have for follow-up as needed.

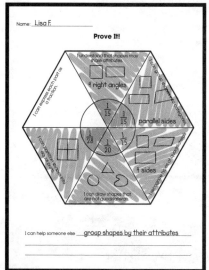

This fun sheet asks students to prove that the statements in the hexagon are true. Have students draw or write their proof of proficiency in the space between the statement and the middle circle. If correct, students should write the date in the center segment of the small circle. Finally, have students color each segment as they master the concept. When the hexagon is filled in completely, have students write one skill they feel good enough about to help others with.

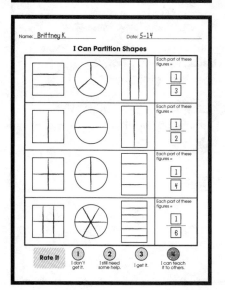

This sheet will allow students to show what they know about partitioning shapes. Give students a directive, such as, "Divide each shape in the top row into three equal parts." Once students have done so, they should fill in the fraction in the right section. Repeat this for all four sections. Then, have students use the 1–4 scale at the bottom to self-assess their performance.

Identifying Shapes

Given Shapes	Date _____
	☐ Can name grade-level shapes
	☐ Can draw grade-level shapes
	☐ Can tell the shared attributes of shapes
	☐ Can classify rhombuses, rectangles, and squares as quadrilaterals
	☐ Can draw examples of quadrilaterals not in these subcategories
	☐ Recommendations

Given Shapes	Date _____
	☐ Can name grade-level shapes
	☐ Can draw grade-level shapes
	☐ Can tell the shared attributes of shapes
	☐ Can classify rhombuses, rectangles, and squares as quadrilaterals
	☐ Can draw examples of quadrilaterals not in these subcategories
	☐ Recommendations

Name: _____

Prove It!

I understand that shapes may share attributes.

I can group shapes into categories.

I can express each part as a fraction.

I recognize types of quadrilaterals.

I can partition shapes into equal parts.

I can draw shapes that are not quadrilaterals.

I can help someone else _____

_____

_____

I Can Partition Shapes

Each part of these figures =

$$\frac{\square}{\square}$$

Each part of these figures =

$$\frac{\square}{\square}$$

Each part of these figures =

$$\frac{\square}{\square}$$

Each part of these figures =

$$\frac{\square}{\square}$$

Reading: Literature Standards Crosswalk

Second Grade

Key Ideas and Details

- Ask and answer questions about key details in a text.
- Recount stories, including fables and folktales from diverse cultures, and determine their central messages, lessons, or morals.
- Describe how characters in a story respond to major events and challenges.

Craft and Structure

- Tell how words and phrases supply rhythm and meaning in a story, poem, or song.
- Describe the overall structure of a story.
- Understand the purpose of a story's beginning and ending.
- Acknowledge differences in the points of view of characters.
- Use different voices for each character when reading dialogue aloud.

Integration of Knowledge and Ideas

- Use information from illustrations and words in text to demonstrate understanding of its characters, setting, or plot.
- Compare and contrast two or more versions of the same story by different authors or from different cultures.

Range of Reading and Level of Text Complexity

- By the end of the year, proficiently read and comprehend literature in the grades 2–3 text complexity band.

Fourth Grade

Key Ideas and Details

- Refer to text details and examples when explaining text and drawing inferences.
- Use text details to determine a theme of a story, drama, or poem.
- Summarize a text.
- Describe a character, setting, or event in depth using specific details from a text.

Craft and Structure

- Determine the meaning of words and phrases in a text.
- Explain major differences between poems, drama, and prose, and refer to the structural elements of poetry and drama when writing or speaking about a text.
- Compare and contrast the points of view of different stories.
- Know the difference between first- and third-person points of view.

Integration of Knowledge and Ideas

- Make connections between a text and a visual or oral presentation of the text.
- Compare and contrast similar themes, topics, and patterns of events in stories, myths, and traditional literature from different cultures.

Range of Reading and Level of Text Complexity

- By the end of the year, proficiently read and comprehend literature in the grades 4–5 text complexity band.

Reading: Literature Concepts Checklist

Concept		Dates Taught				

Reading Comprehension: Literature

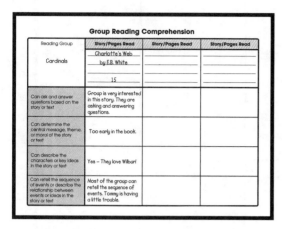

Use this form to keep track of a reading group's comprehension of a specific text or texts. Record the group name. Then, write the chapter title or book name in the top sections as you read the selections. Keep track of observations based on the group discussion, participation, enjoyment, and comprehension in the boxes below according to the skills listed in the left-hand column.

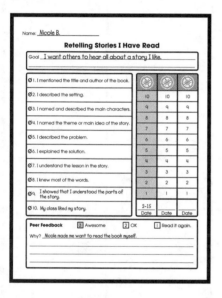

Have students use this form to assess their own progress on retelling three different stories to peers. Before starting, have students write a goal about retelling a story. Numbers 9 and 10 are left blank to allow you or the student to add other specific skills. After peers have listened, they should offer feedback by rating the storyteller and supporting the rating with a reason. If a student tries this with three different people, have the peer reviewers sign their names and use different colors of pens in their writing and rating.

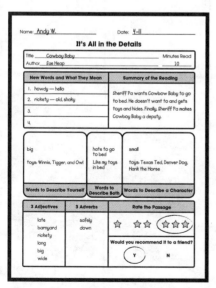

Use this form to assess a student's comprehension of a single book or story. First, have students write the title of the piece, author's name, and how many minutes they spent reading it. Have students list new words and brief summaries next. In the middle diagram, have students describe themselves in the left box, the main character in the right box, and characteristics in common in the middle box. Then, have them list adjectives and adverbs in the bottom-left boxes. Finally, have students rate the piece and say whether they would recommend it to a friend.

Group Reading Comprehension

Story/Pages Read	Story/Pages Read	Story/Pages Read	
			Can ask and answer questions based on the story or text
			Can determine the central message, theme, or moral of the story or text
			Can describe the characters or key ideas in the story or text
			Can retell the sequence of events or describe the relationship between events or ideas in the story or text

Name: _____

Retelling Stories I Have Read

Goal _____
_____

○ 1. I mentioned the title and author of the book.	☀	☀	☀
○ 2. I described the setting.	10	10	10
○ 3. I named and described the main characters.	9	9	9
	8	8	8
○ 4. I named the theme or main idea of the story.	7	7	7
○ 5. I described the problem.	6	6	6
○ 6. I explained the solution.	5	5	5
	4	4	4
○ 7. I understand the lesson in the story.	3	3	3
○ 8. I knew most of the words.	2	2	2
○ 9.	1	1	1
○ 10.	___ Date	___ Date	___ Date

Peer Feedback   3 Awesome   2 OK   1 Read it again.

Why? _____
_____
_____
_____

Name: _____   Date: _____

It's All in the Details

Title _____ Minutes Read

Author _____ _____

New Words and What They Mean	Summary of the Reading
1.	
2.	
3.	
4.	

Words to Describe Yourself

Words to Describe Both

Words to Describe a Character

3 Adjectives	3 Adverbs	Rate the Passage
		☆ ☆☆ ☆☆☆
		Would you recommend it to a friend? Y N

Stories, Dramas, and Poems

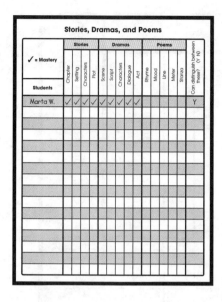

Use this page to record your students' proficiency with prose, poetry, and drama terms and skills. Using either formal or informal assessments, place a check mark to record individual student proficiencies for each skill or term. Check the last column to the right when students can distinguish between the three. (Note: *Rhyme* can refer to identifying rhymes or rhyme schemes.)

Use this page to assess your students' abilities to differentiate between the three main forms of literature. Provide or have students choose a piece of literature. Have students write the title and author's name in the spaces provided. Then, have students circle the type of literature and complete the reasoning section to explain their choices. Finally, have students date and rate their work in the box at the bottom of each section, using the 1–4 scale provided. In the *Notes* section, have students note questions or make comments.

This form will allow students to show that they know the difference between a poem and a play by asking them to offer examples of the structural elements of each. Provide or have students choose a poem and a play to analyze. Before they read either, have students write the title and author. Ask them to look for examples of each element as they read. When they think they understand the element and have given appropriate examples, students should place a check mark in the check box.

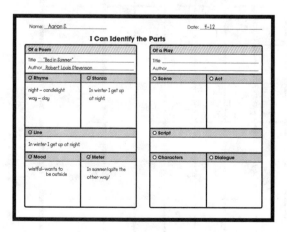

Stories, Dramas, and Poems

✓ = Mastery / Students	Stories				Dramas					Poems					Can distinguish between these? (Y N)
	Chapter	Setting	Characters	Plot	Scene	Script	Characters	Dialogue	Act	Rhyme	Mood	Line	Meter	Stanza	

Name: _____

Identifying Stories, Dramas, and Poems

| Title _____ | Title _____ |
| Author _____ | Author _____ |

story	**drama**	**poem**

I know because _____

_____

_____

_____

_____.

Date _____

| Title _____ | Title _____ |
| Author _____ | Author _____ |

story	**drama**	**poem**

I know because _____

_____

_____

_____

_____.

Date _____

Notes

_____

_____

_____

 Rate It

 1 I don't get it.

2 I still need some help.

 3 I get it.

 4 I can teach it to others.

Name: _____

Date: _____

I Can Identify the Parts

Of a Poem

Title _____

Author _____

O Stanza	
O Rhyme	

O Line	O Meter
O Mood	

Of a Play

Title _____

Author _____

O Act	
O Scene	

O Script	O Dialogue
O Characters	

Story Elements

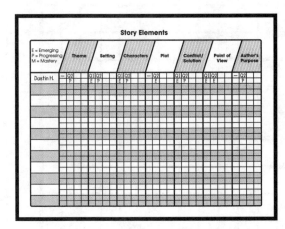

Use this page to record each student's understanding of all story element concepts. Record student names in the left column. For each concept, record an assessment of a student's progress four times throughout the year, such as quarterly. Record the date at the top of each column and the level of proficiency below using a system of your choosing, such as check marks, or the *E*, *P*, and *M* system shown.

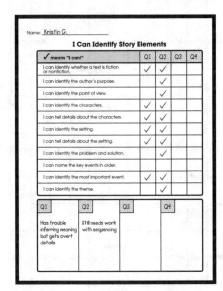

This page makes a good conferencing sheet and will help students track their progress throughout a unit or across the entire year. You or students may record dates in the four top spaces to the right each time you assess. After you first address the story elements, have students rate their understanding by placing check marks beside the statements that are true. Discuss each one to ascertain students' understanding. Use the bottom section to list observations and recommendations for follow-up. Repeat until you observe mastery.

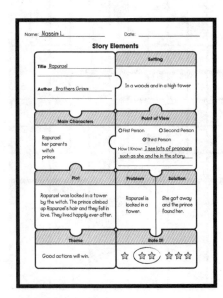

Provide this page to students to use as a book report form. After students have completed a book, they should write the details of the book according to the given prompts. Use the page as another gauge of students' understanding of story elements. If desired, store the completed page with a student's assessment data form, such as the one shown on page 80.

Story Elements

	Theme	Setting	Characters	Plot	Conflict/Solution	Point of View	Author's Purpose

E = Emerging
P = Progressing
M = Mastery

Name: _____

I Can Identify Story Elements

✔ means "I can!"				
I can identify whether a text is fiction or nonfiction.				
I can identify the author's purpose.				
I can identify the point of view.				
I can identify the characters.				
I can tell details about the characters.				
I can identify the setting.				
I can tell details about the setting.				
I can identify the problem and solution.				
I can name the key events in order.				
I can identify the most important event.				
I can identify the theme.				

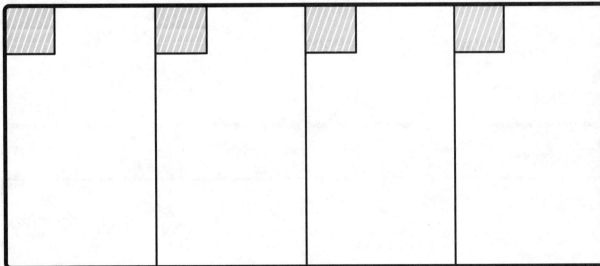

Story Elements

Title _____
_____

Author _____
_____

Setting

Main Characters

Point of View

O First Person   O Second Person

O Third Person

How I Know: _____
_____
_____

Plot

Problem   Solution

Theme

Rate It!

☆ ☆☆ ☆☆☆

Reading: Informational Text Standards Crosswalk

Second Grade

Key Ideas and Details

- Ask and answer questions about key details in a text.
- Identify the main topic of a text and the focus of specific paragraphs.
- Describe the connection between a series of historic events, scientific ideas or concepts, or steps in technical procedures in a text.

Craft and Structure

- Determine the meaning of words and phrases in a text.
- Use text features (captions, bold print, subheadings, glossaries, indexes, electronic menus, icons) to locate information.
- Identify the main purpose of a text, including the author's purpose.

Integration of Knowledge and Ideas

- Explain how specific images contribute to and clarify a text.
- Describe how reasons support specific points made in a text.
- Compare and contrast key points presented by two texts on the same topic.

Reading and Level of Text Complexity

- By the end of the year, read and comprehend informational texts in the grades 2-3 complexity band.

Fourth Grade

Key Ideas and Details

- Refer to text details and examples when explaining text and drawing inferences.
- Determine the main idea of a text using key details.
- Summarize a text.
- Explain events, procedures, ideas, or concepts in a historical, scientific, or technical text, including what happened and why, based on specific information.
- Determine the meaning of general academic and domain-specific words or phrases in a grade 4 text.
- Describe the overall structure of events, ideas, concepts, or information in a text.
- Compare and contrast a firsthand and secondhand account of the same event or topic, including the focus and the information provided.

Integration of Knowledge and Ideas

- Interpret information presented visually, orally, or quantitatively and explain how it contributes to an understanding of the text.
- Explain how an author uses reasons and evidence to support text points.
- Integrate information from two texts on the same topic to write or speak knowledgeably about the subject.

Range of Reading and Level of Text Complexity

- By the end of year, read and comprehend informational texts in the grades 4–5 text complexity band proficiently.

Reading: Informational Text Concepts Checklist

Concept	Dates Taught			

Reading Comprehension: Informational Text

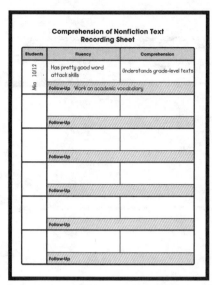

Use this form to get a snapshot look at the reading fluency and comprehension or your students or a reading group. Keep the form on a clipboard and make notes as you observe students reading nonfiction text. Add any recommendations for improvement or strengths that you observe.

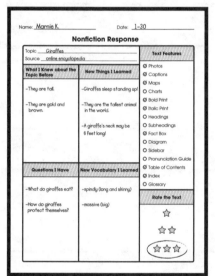

This page allows students to analyze a text they have read (online or off) and to show their understanding of text features. Have students record the title and source of a text they have recently read. Next, have students analyze the text in the four large boxes. Then, have students complete a text feature scavenger hunt by checking off the text features they find in the source material. Finally, have students rate the text by circling one, two, or three stars.

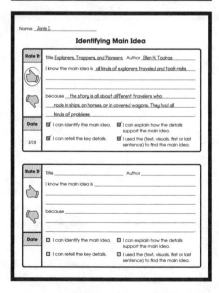

Use this form again and again to help students identify the main idea of different books. Have students keep a record of the nonfiction texts they've read by filling out this form with each. Have them record the name and author (or source). Have them identify the main idea and explain why they think it is the main idea. Then, have students place a check mark in the boxes next to true statements about their proficiency. Finally, have students write the date and rate the book in the left-hand column.

Comprehension of Nonfiction Text
Recording Sheet

Students	Fluency	Comprehension
	Follow-Up	
	Follow-Up	
	Follow-Up	
	Follow-Up	
	Follow-Up	
	Follow-Up	

Name: _____   Date: _____

Nonfiction Response

Topic _____

Source _____

What I Knew about the Topic Before	New Things I Learned

Questions I Have	New Vocabulary I Learned

Text Features

O Photos

O Captions

O Maps

O Charts

O Bold Print

O Italic Print

O Headings

O Subheadings

O Fact Box

O Diagram

O Sidebar

O Pronunciation Guide

O Table of Contents

O Index

O Glossary

Rate the Text

☆

☆ ☆

☆ ☆ ☆

Identifying Main Idea

Rate It	

Rate It

Title _____ Author _____

I know the main idea is _____

_____

_____

because _____

_____

_____.

Date

☐ I can identify the main idea. ☐ I can explain how the details support the main idea.

☐ I can retell the key details. ☐ I used the (text, visuals, first or last sentence) to find the main idea.

Rate It

Title _____ Author _____

I know the main idea is _____

_____

_____

because _____

_____

_____.

Date

☐ I can identify the main idea. ☐ I can explain how the details support the main idea.

☐ I can retell the key details. ☐ I used the (text, visuals, first or last sentence) to find the main idea.

Academic Vocabulary

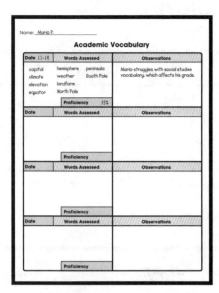

Students need to learn the vocabulary of the content areas to understand the content. As you pre-teach unit vocabulary, use this form to keep track of the words you have taught and assessed. Use the *Observations* section to note learning behaviors and follow-up plans.

Use this form as students encounter unfamiliar words. Have students write the word in the top left space, then skip to the bottom-right space (beside *Before*) to rate how well they already know it. They may use any strategy to figure out the word's meaning and write it in the *Definition* box. Next, have them draw a picture to represent the word or remind themselves of its meaning. Then, have them write a synonym and antonym for the word and use the word in a sentence. Finally, have students return to the bottom right and rate how well they understand the word now.

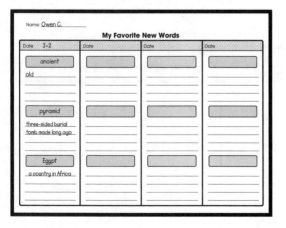

Assess students' individual knowledge of vocabulary with this page. Have students record their favorite new words and provide definitions or sentences using the words to prove understanding. You may choose to have students record new words quarterly or at the end of a unit. Keep this page as a record of learning throughout the year.

Name: _____

Academic Vocabulary

Date	Words Assessed	Observations
	Proficiency	

Date	Words Assessed	Observations
	Proficiency	

Date	Words Assessed	Observations
	Proficiency	

Date	Words Assessed	Observations
	Proficiency	

Words That Help Me in School

Word	Picture

Definition

Synonym(s) | **Antonym(s)**

How well do I know it?

	★	★★★	★★★★
Before			
After			

Sentence

Word	Picture

Definition

Synonym(s) | **Antonym(s)**

How well do I know it?

	★	★★★	★★★★
Before			
After			

Sentence

Name: _____

My Favorite New Words

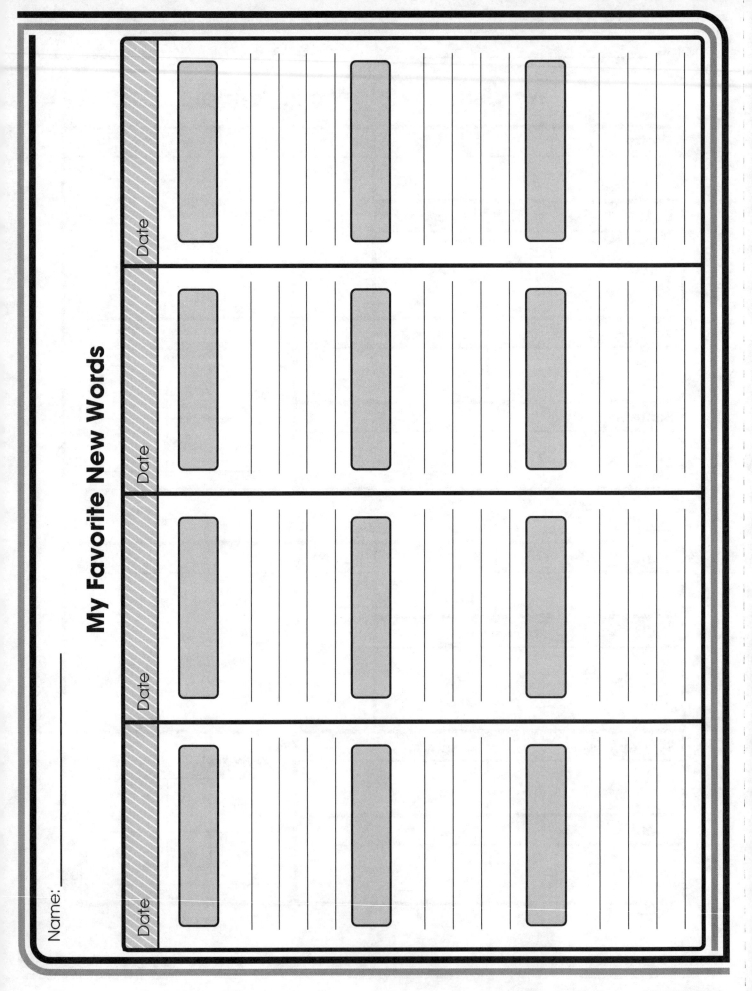

Date

Date

Date

Date

Reading Logs

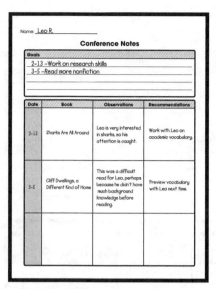

Use this form to confer with students about each completed text for fiction or nonfiction texts. Write and discuss a goal during each meeting with each student. Then, write the date of the conference and the name of the book that you discussed. In the *Observations* column, write compliments and brief notes. Finally, note any follow-up plans or goals in the *Recommendations* column.

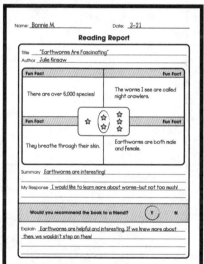

Have students use this reading report form after reading any text (fiction or nonfiction). These can be saved over the span of the school year. Have students fill in the title and author or source of the text, followed by four fun facts they learned. Then, have them write a summary of the text, offer a brief response to the text, and explain whether they would or would not recommend it to a friend. Finally, have students rate the text by circling one, two, or three stars in the middle of the *Fun Fact* boxes.

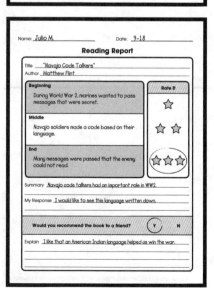

Have students use this reading log to track their independent fiction or nonfiction reading. After students have read appropriate and self-selected books independently, have students fill in the title of the book and its author. Have them write the beginning, middle, and end of the text. Then, have them explain whether they would recommend the text to a friend and explain why. Finally, have students rate the books by giving them one, two, or three stars. Note: If this was a take-home assignment, ask family members to initial the page before returning it to school.

Name: _____

Conference Notes

Goals

Date	Book	Observations	Recommendations

Name: _____   Date: _____

Reading Report

Title _____

Author _____

Fun Fact	Fun Fact

☆ ☆ ☆
☆ ☆
☆

Fun Fact	Fun Fact

Summary _____

_____

My Response _____

_____

Would you recommend the book to a friend?   Y   N

Explain _____

_____

_____

_____

Name: _____   Date: _____

Reading Report

Title _____

Author _____

Beginning

Middle

End

Rate It

☆

☆ ☆

☆ ☆ ☆

Summary _____

_____

My Response _____

_____

Would you recommend the book to a friend?   **Y**   **N**

Explain _____

_____

_____

Reading: Foundational Skills
Standards Crosswalk

Second Grade

Print Concepts and Phonological Awareness end in first grade.

Phonics and Word Recognition

- Know and apply grade-level phonics and word analysis skills.
- Identify long and short vowels in regularly spelled one-syllable words.
- Know spelling-sound correspondences for additional common vowel teams.
- Decode regularly spelled two-syllable words with long vowels.
- Decode words with common prefixes and suffixes.
- Identify words with inconsistent but common spelling-sound correspondences.
- Recognize and read grade-appropriate irregularly spelled words.

Fluency

- Read with sufficient accuracy and fluency to support comprehension.
- Read grade-level text with purpose and understanding.
- Read grade-level text orally with accuracy, appropriate rate, and expression on successive readings.
- Use context and rereading to confirm or self-correct word recognition and understanding.

Fourth Grade

Phonics and Word Recognition

- Know and apply grade-level phonics and word analysis skills in decoding words.
- Use combined knowledge of all letter-sound correspondences, syllabication patterns, and roots and affixes to accurately read unfamiliar multisyllabic words.

Fluency

- Read with sufficient accuracy and fluency to support comprehension.
- Read grade-level text with purpose and understanding.
- Read grade-level prose and poetry orally with accuracy, appropriate rate, and expression on successive readings.
- Use context and rereading to confirm or self-correct word recognition and understanding.

Reading: Foundational Skills Concepts Checklist

Concept		Dates Taught				

Decoding

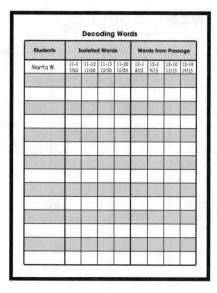

Use this form to track individual student progress and proficiency with decoding words. As you assess students when they are decoding isolated words or reading a passage, record the date and the number of correct words over the total words assessed. This form allows you to assess each student up to four times a year.

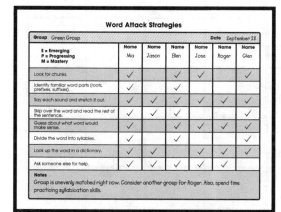

Observing students as they engage in literacy activities can help you plan subsequent lessons. Reading groups provide a perfect opportunity. Use this simple sheet to focus on the word attack strategies your students use. Fill in the name of the group and each member's name. If you have more than six students in a group, divide one or more of the student columns in half. Place check marks under names as you observe mastery. Use the **Notes** section to record any observations or recommendations.

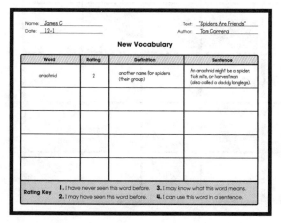

Have students use this form to track new vocabulary. One sheet covers one book. Keep copies in students' portfolio. Have students write the title and author in the top right. Each time students read an unknown word, have them write it in the first column and then rate it using the 1–4 rating scale at the bottom. After defining a word, have students use it in a sentence. Students may peruse these forms later in the year to see if the words are still unfamiliar or by then part of their vocabularies.

Decoding Words

Students	Isolated Words			Words from Passage		

Word Attack Strategies

Group	Name	Name	Name	Name	Name	Name	
E = Emerging **P = Progressing** **M = Mastery**							
Look for chunks.							
Identify familiar word parts (roots, prefixes, suffixes).							
Say each sound and stretch it out.							
Skip over the word and read the rest of the sentence.							
Guess about what word would make sense.							
Divide the word into syllables.							
Look up the word in a dictionary.							
Ask someone else for help.							
Notes							

Date

Name: _____

Date: _____

Author: _____

Text: _____

New Vocabulary

Word	Rating	Definition	Sentence

Rating Key

1. I have never seen this word before.

2. I may have seen this word before.

3. I may know what this word means.

4. I can use this word in a sentence.

Fluency

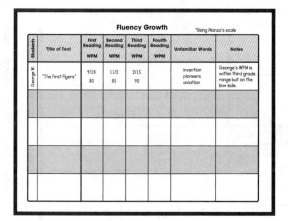

Use this page to record a student's proficiency with fluency throughout the year. Record student names in the left column. The form allows you to record an assessment of each student's progress four times. Record the date at the top of each section. Then, record the level of proficiency for each part of fluency (**E**xpression, **R**ate, **P**hrasing, and **A**ccuracy) using a system of your choosing. Use the large box to record any observations or to note a student's proficiency with comprehension as well.

Use this form to track students' progress in reading fluency. You can test students yourself or teach students how to time each other in a partner activity. Record each student's name in the left-hand column. In the *Title of Text* column, write one title if you use the same text each time. If you use a different text each time, write the date and each title. Write the date and words per minute (WPM) in each space as you test. Note any unfamiliar words. Use the *Notes* section to record observations.

This page will allow students to monitor and self-assess their own fluency as they read. You may also send copies home so that family members can help assess progress. Have students record the title and the time it took them to read a given passage. Then, have students rate themselves on each skill by circling a number. Allow students to choose a focus for next time. You may also use this page to have partners assess each other.

Oral Fluency

Name	E = Expression	R = Rate	P = Phrasing	A = Accuracy

	Date			Date		
	E	R		E	R	
	P	A		P	A	
	Date			Date		
	E	R		E	R	
	P	A		P	A	
	Date			Date		
	E	R		E	R	
	P	A		P	A	
	Date			Date		
	E	R		E	R	
	P	A		P	A	
	Date			Date		
	E	R		E	R	
	P	A		P	A	
	Date			Date		
	E	R		E	R	
	P	A		P	A	

Fluency Growth

Students	Title of Text	First Reading WPM	Second Reading WPM	Third Reading WPM	Fourth Reading WPM	Unfamiliar Words	Notes

Name: _____ Date: _____

Fluency Self-Assessment

Title _____ Time _____min. _____sec.

Expression I changed my voice to match the words.	1	2	3	4
Rate My speed was not too fast or too slow.	1	2	3	4
Phrasing I paused at the correct times.	1	2	3	4
Accuracy I said the words correctly.	1	2	3	4

Focus for Next Time _____

Name: _____ Date: _____

Fluency Self-Assessment

Title _____ Time _____min. _____sec.

Expression I changed my voice to match the words.	1	2	3	4
Rate My speed was not too fast or too slow.	1	2	3	4
Phrasing I paused at the correct times.	1	2	3	4
Accuracy I said the words correctly.	1	2	3	4

Focus for Next Time _____

Writing Standards Crosswalk

Second Grade

Text Types and Purposes

- Write opinion pieces that introduce a topic or book, state an opinion, supply reasons, use linking words, and provide a concluding statement or section.
- Write informative/explanatory texts that introduce a topic, use facts and definitions to develop points, and provide a concluding statement or section.
- Write narratives that recount a detailed event or short sequence of events; include details to describe actions, thoughts, and feelings; use temporal words to signal event order; and provide a sense of closure.

Production and Distribution of Writing

With guidance and support:

- Focus on a topic and strengthen writing as needed by revising and editing.
- Use a variety of digital tools to produce and publish writing, including with peers.

Research to Build and Present Knowledge

- Participate in shared research and writing projects.
- Recall information or gather information from sources to answer a question.

Fourth Grade

Text Types and Purposes

- Write opinion pieces, supporting a point of view with reasons and information.
- Introduce a topic clearly, state an opinion, and group related ideas; provide reasons supported by facts and details; use linking words and phrases; provide a conclusion related to the opinion.
- Write informative/explanatory texts to examine a topic and convey ideas and information clearly.
- Group related information; include formatting, illustrations, and multimedia when useful; develop a topic with facts, definitions, details, quotations, and other relevant information; use linking words and phrases to connect ideas; provide a concluding statement or section related to the information presented.
- Write narratives using effective technique, details, and clear sequences.
- Establish a situation; introduce a narrator and/or characters; organize a natural event sequence; use dialogue and description; use concrete words, phrases, and sensory details; provide a conclusion.

Production and Distribution of Writing

- Produce coherent writing with development and organization that is appropriate to task and purpose.
- With guidance and support, develop and strengthen writing as needed by planning, revising, and editing.
- Use technology to produce and publish writing as well as to interact and collaborate with others.
- Demonstrate sufficient keyboarding skills to type at least one page in a sitting.

Research to Build and Present Knowledge

- Conduct short research projects that build knowledge about a topic's various aspects.
- Recall relevant information from experiences or gather information from print and digital sources.
- Take notes, categorize information, and provide a list of sources.
- Draw evidence from texts to support analysis, reflection, and research.

Range of Writing

- Write routinely over time for a range of discipline-specific tasks, purposes, and audiences.

Writing Concepts Checklist

	Concept	Dates Taught			

Opinion Writing

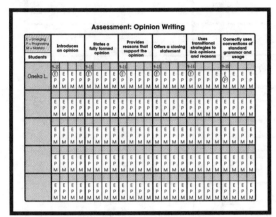

Use this sheet to track a student's proficiencies in writing. You may also easily modify the sheet to track other types of writing. Record each student's name in the left column. Under each skill are four spaces for recording dates of different writing work. Record the date and circle the level of progress. With this information at your fingertips, you can track students' progress and their strengths and weaknesses.

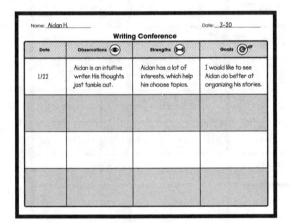

It's very important to begin a writing conference with a positive affirmation for the student, a statement of strengths to build on, and goals for upcoming writing projects. This sheet has it all laid out, with plenty of room for observations. Use the sheet to keep track of writing progress for as long as or as often as needed. Record the date in the left-hand column. Write your comments in the subsequent columns. For end-of-the-year conferences, attach copies of the writing pieces these comments covered.

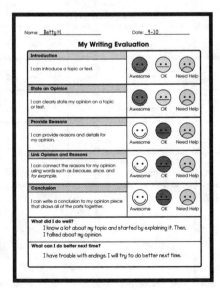

Use this sheet to evaluate students on various writing projects throughout the year. Have students use it to organize their work and to check their writing when finished. Have students color or circle a face next to each skill to show how well they did. In the bottom two boxes, have students write short statements about something they did well and something they can do better next time.

Assessment: Opinion Writing

E = Emerging
P = Progressing
M = Mastery

Students	Introduces an opinion	States a fully formed opinion	Provides reasons that support the opinion	Offers a closing statement	Uses transitional strategies to link opinions and reasons	Correctly uses conventions of standard grammar and usage
	E P M	E P M	E P M	E P M	E P M	E P M
	E P M	E P M	E P M	E P M	E P M	E P M
	E P M	E P M	E P M	E P M	E P M	E P M
	E P M	E P M	E P M	E P M	E P M	E P M
	E P M	E P M	E P M	E P M	E P M	E P M

Name: _____   Date: _____

Writing Conference

Date	Observations 👁	Strengths 🏋	Goals 🎯

Name: _____ Date: _____

My Writing Evaluation

Introduction	
I can introduce a topic or text.	 Awesome OK Need Help

State an Opinion	
I can clearly state my opinion on a topic or text.	 Awesome OK Need Help

Provide Reasons	
I can provide reasons and details for my opinion.	 Awesome OK Need Help

Link Opinion and Reasons	
I can connect the reasons for my opinion using words such as *because, since,* and *for example*.	 Awesome OK Need Help

Conclusion	
I can write a conclusion to my opinion piece that draws all of the parts together.	 Awesome OK Need Help

What did I do well?

What can I do better next time?

Informative Writing

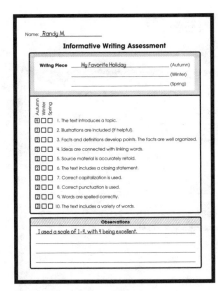

Use this sheet to track students' progress and pinpoint their strengths and weaknesses throughout the year. You may find it useful to attach copies of each piece of writing to the skill assessment sheet so that examples are at your fingertips. For each student, write the names of each piece of writing at the top. Mark your assessment of the student's writing skills in the boxes with the rating scale of your choice. This example shows a scale of 1 to 4, with 4 being mastery. Note your observations at the bottom. You may add another page of notes if necessary.

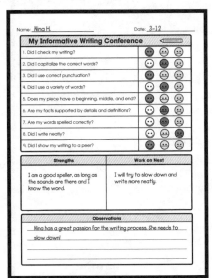

Use this form during a student writing conference regarding a particular piece of writing. Read the piece together and point out the good points and any errors. Then, allow the student to rate herself by coloring or circling the appropriate face. Have the student fill in the next two boxes by writing a sentence about what she has done well and what she can do better next time. Note your observations at the bottom, including a compliment and a goal.

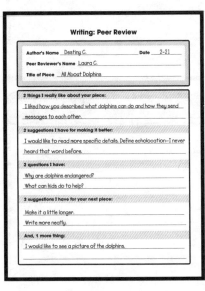

Peer reviews can be quite useful in helping students to improve their work. Closely monitor the activity to ensure that students are respectful of each other's feelings. If accepted, this constructive feedback will help writers revise and improve their work. Have each peer reviewer complete this sheet. It should include the author's name, date, peer reviewer's name, and title at the top. After reading the piece, the peer reviewer should complete the rest of the sheet with thoughtful and honest statements. For future reference, attach a copy of the writing piece to the peer review sheet.

Name: _____

Informative Writing Assessment

Writing Piece _____ (Autumn)

_____ (Winter)

_____ (Spring)

Autumn Winter Spring

☐ ☐ ☐ 1. The text introduces a topic.

☐ ☐ ☐ 2. Illustrations are included (if helpful).

☐ ☐ ☐ 3. Facts and definitions develop points. The facts are well organized.

☐ ☐ ☐ 4. Ideas are connected with linking words.

☐ ☐ ☐ 5. Source material is accurately retold.

☐ ☐ ☐ 6. The text includes a closing statement.

☐ ☐ ☐ 7. Correct capitalization is used.

☐ ☐ ☐ 8. Correct punctuation is used.

☐ ☐ ☐ 9. Words are spelled correctly.

☐ ☐ ☐ 10. The text includes a variety of words.

Observations

_____

_____

_____

_____

Name: _____ Date: _____

My Informative Writing Conference ✏️

1. Did I check my writing?	🙂 😐 🙁
2. Did I capitalize the correct words?	🙂 😐 🙁
3. Did I use correct punctuation?	🙂 😐 🙁
4. Did I use a variety of words?	🙂 😐 🙁
5. Does my piece have a beginning, middle, and end?	🙂 😐 🙁
6. Are my facts supported by details and definitions?	🙂 😐 🙁
7. Are my words spelled correctly?	🙂 😐 🙁
8. Did I write neatly?	🙂 😐 🙁
9. Did I show my writing to a peer?	🙂 😐 🙁

Strengths	Work on Next

Observations

_____

_____

_____

_____

Writing: Peer Review

Author's Name _____ Date _____

Peer Reviewer's Name _____

Title of Piece _____

2 things I really like about your piece:

_____

_____

2 suggestions I have for making it better:

_____

_____

2 questions I have:

_____

_____

2 suggestions I have for your next piece:

_____

_____

And, 1 more thing:

_____

_____

Narrative Writing

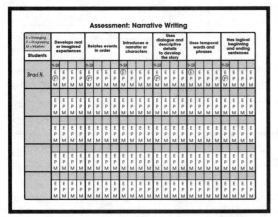

Use this sheet to track students' growing writing skills. You may easily modify the sheet to track other types of writing. Record each student's name in the left column. Below each skill are four spaces for recording dates of different writing work. Record the date and circle the level of progress. With this information at your fingertips, you can track students' progress and their strengths and weaknesses.

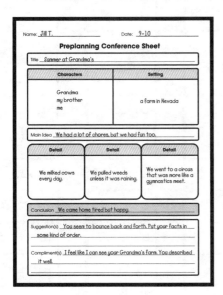

Use this conference sheet to give students feedback during the preplanning stage of writing a story. Ask students to spend time planning and filling out the *Title*, *Characters*, *Setting*, *Main Idea*, three *Details*, and *Conclusion*. In the conference setting, allow students to share their thoughts about their stories, using their notes. Talk about the story, ask questions, and then record any suggestions and compliments in the spaces at the bottom of the sheet.

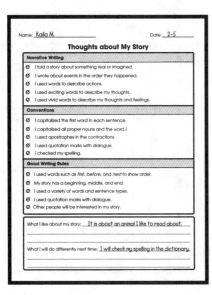

This form makes it easy for students to assess themselves on their narrative writing skills. They need only check off the boxes for the skills they think they mastered in their narratives. You may also introduce this form before the writing lesson to remind students of the skills they should use. After checking off the appropriate boxes, have students write a sentence or two to explain what they like about their stories and what they will do differently next time. Be sure to attach a copy of the narrative writing piece to this form.

Assessment: Narrative Writing

E = Emerging
P = Progressing
M = Mastery

Students	Develops real or imagined experiences				Relates events in order				Introduces a narrator or characters				Uses dialogue and descriptive details to develop the story				Uses temporal words and phrases				Has logical beginning and ending sentences			
	E P M	E P M	E P M	E P M	E P M	E P M	E P M	E P M	E P M	E P M	E P M	E P M	E P M	E P M	E P M	E P M	E P M	E P M	E P M	E P M	E P M	E P M	E P M	E P M
	E P M	E P M	E P M	E P M	E P M	E P M	E P M	E P M	E P M	E P M	E P M	E P M	E P M	E P M	E P M	E P M	E P M	E P M	E P M	E P M	E P M	E P M	E P M	E P M
	E P M	E P M	E P M	E P M	E P M	E P M	E P M	E P M	E P M	E P M	E P M	E P M	E P M	E P M	E P M	E P M	E P M	E P M	E P M	E P M	E P M	E P M	E P M	E P M
	E P M	E P M	E P M	E P M	E P M	E P M	E P M	E P M	E P M	E P M	E P M	E P M	E P M	E P M	E P M	E P M	E P M	E P M	E P M	E P M	E P M	E P M	E P M	E P M
	E P M	E P M	E P M	E P M	E P M	E P M	E P M	E P M	E P M	E P M	E P M	E P M	E P M	E P M	E P M	E P M	E P M	E P M	E P M	E P M	E P M	E P M	E P M	E P M

Name: _____   Date: _____

Preplanning Conference Sheet

Title _____

Characters	Setting

Main Idea _____

Detail	Detail	Detail

Conclusion _____

Suggestion(s) _____

_____

_____

Compliment(s) _____

_____

_____

Name: _____   Date: _____

Thoughts about My Story

Narrative Writing

- ○ I told a story about something real or imagined.
- ○ I wrote about events in the order they happened.
- ○ I used words to describe actions.
- ○ I used exciting words to describe my thoughts.
- ○ I used vivid words to describe my thoughts and feelings.

Conventions

- ○ I capitalized the first word in each sentence.
- ○ I capitalized all proper nouns and the word *I*.
- ○ I used apostrophes in the contractions.
- ○ I used quotation marks with dialogue.
- ○ I checked my spelling.

Good Writing Rules

- ○ I used words such as *first*, *before*, and *next* to show order.
- ○ My story has a beginning, middle, and end.
- ○ I used a variety of words and sentence types.
- ○ I used quotation marks with dialogue.
- ○ Other people will be interested in my story.

What I like about my story: _____
_____
_____

What I will do differently next time: _____
_____
_____

Revising and Editing

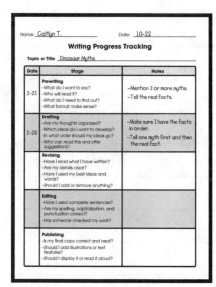

Use this page to record your students' proficiency with revising and editing tasks. Use either formal or informal assessments and a scale of your choosing (or the *E*, *P*, and *M* scale shown here) to record individual student proficiencies and dates assessed for each task.

Allow students to use this progress-tracking page to guide a piece of writing through the entire process. Have students record the title or topic of the piece at the top. As students reach each stage, have them add the date and use the questions in the *Stage* section to guide their thinking. Students may use the *Notes* section to add any relevant thoughts or reminders. If desired, use this page as part of your writing conferencing to help students become comfortable with the practice.

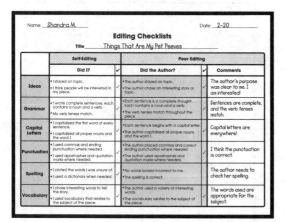

This sheet will encourage students to edit and revise their writing. It includes the added component of peer review. Have students write their names and the date at the top and then the title of their writing. Next, have students pair with peers. Monitor interactions to ensure that students are respectful of each other's feelings. After reading the piece, the peer reviewer should make appropriate comments in the right column.

Revising and Editing

E = Emerging P = Progressing M = Mastery	Revising				Editing			
Students	Clarity and Focus	Organization	Word Choice	Supporting Details	Capitalization	Punctuation	Spelling	Grammar

Name: _____   Date: _____

Writing Progress Tracking

Topic or Title _____

Date	Stage	Notes
	Prewriting –What do I want to say? –Who will read it? –What do I need to find out? –What format make sense?	
	Drafting –Are my thoughts organized? –Which ideas do I want to develop? –In what order should my ideas go? –Who can read this and offer suggestions?	
	Revising –Have I read what I have written? –Are my details clear? –Have I used my best ideas and words? –Should I add or remove anything?	
	Editing –Have I used complete sentences? –Are my spelling, capitalization, and punctuation correct? –Has someone checked my work?	
	Publishing –Is my final copy correct and neat? –Should I add illustrations or text features? –Should I display it or read it aloud?	

Name: _____

Date: _____

Editing Checklists

Title _____

	Self-Editing			Peer Editing		
	Did I?	✔		**Did the Author?**	✔	**Comments**
Ideas	• I stayed on topic. • I think people will be interested in my piece.			• The author stayed on topic. • The author chose an interesting story or topic.		
Grammar	• I wrote complete sentences; each contains a noun and a verb. • My verb tenses match.			• Each sentence is a complete thought. Each contains a noun and a verb. • The verb tenses match throughout the piece.		
Capital Letters	• I capitalized the first word of every sentence. • I capitalized all proper nouns and the word *I*.			• Each sentence begins with a capital letter. • The author capitalized all proper nouns and the word *I*.		
Punctuation	• I used commas and ending punctuation where needed. • I used apostrophes and quotation marks where needed.			• The author placed commas and correct ending punctuation where needed. • The author used apostrophes and quotation marks where needed.		
Spelling	• I circled the words I was unsure of. • I used a dictionary when needed.			• No words looked incorrect to me. • The spelling is correct.		
Vocabulary	• I chose interesting words to tell the story. • I used vocabulary that relates to the subject of the piece.			• The author used a variety of interesting words. • The vocabulary relates to the subject of the piece.		

Speaking and Listening Standards Crosswalk

Second Grade

Comprehension and Collaboration

- Participate in group discussions about grade-appropriate topics and texts.
- Follow agreed-upon discussion rules.
- Comment on the remarks of others and ask for clarification if needed.
- Recount or describe key ideas or details from a text or other channels of information.
- Ask and answer questions about a presentation to clarify comprehension, gather more information, or deepen understanding.

Presentation of Knowledge and Ideas

- Audibly and coherently tell a story or recount an experience with appropriate facts and relevant, descriptive details.
- Create audio recordings of stories or poems.
- Add drawings or other visual displays when appropriate.
- Produce complete sentences to provide requested detail or clarification.

Fourth Grade

Comprehension and Collaboration

- Actively participate in collaborative discussions on grade 4 topics and texts, building on others' ideas and expressing their own clearly.
- Prepare for discussions, using that preparation to explore ideas under discussion.
- Follow agreed-upon rules for discussions and carry out assigned roles.
- Ask and answer questions to clarify information presented, contribute to the conversation, and link comments to others' remarks.
- Explain their ideas and understanding in light of the discussion.
- Paraphrase a text read aloud or other channels of information.
- Identify the reasons and evidence a speaker provides to support particular points.

Presentation of Knowledge and Ideas

- Report on a topic or text, tell a story, or recount an experience in an organized manner, with appropriate facts and descriptive details.
- Speak clearly at an understandable pace.
- Add audio and visual displays when appropriate.
- Differentiate between contexts that need formal and informal English.

Speaking and Listening Concepts Checklist

Concept		Dates Taught				

Speaking and Listening

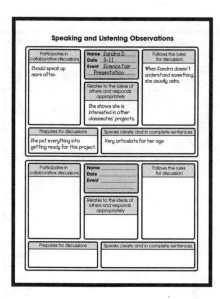

Use this form to track any kind of interaction: peer conversations, student presentations, and small or large group discussions. The top middle box allows you to differentiate between students and events. The page offers opportunities to observe the same student twice. Or, you may wish to track two students on the same page. Keep these sheets on a clipboard as you observe such events. That will make it easy to take notes on different students at once. Write notes in the relevant boxes as you observe students.

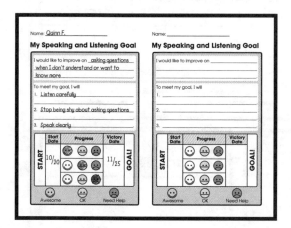

Provide this page to students for setting goals for speaking and listening skills. During individual conferences, work with each student to choose an appropriate goal and complete the prompts. Record the start date at the bottom of the page. Meet regularly to assess and record progress by circling the appropriate symbol. The page includes space for three ratings. Finally, record the date when each student achieves his goal.

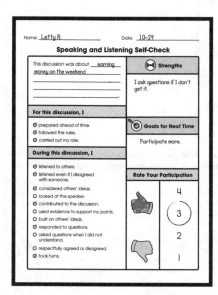

Use this page to help students self-assess their performance in discussions or other group settings. Have students check off the items they did during the discussion. Note that the second set of check boxes is divided into listening skills (top) and speaking skills (bottom). Have students record their strengths and goals for next time in the right-hand sections and then rate their overall performance by shading the appropriate hand and circling a number (with 1 being poor and 4 being outstanding).

Speaking and Listening Observations

Participates in collaborative discussions	Name _____ Date _____ Event _____ _____	Follows the rules for discussion
	Relates to the ideas of others and responds appropriately	

Prepares for discussions	Speaks clearly and in complete sentences

Participates in collaborative discussions	Name _____ Date _____ Event _____ _____	Follows the rules for discussion
	Relates to the ideas of others and responds appropriately	

Prepares for discussions	Speaks clearly and in complete sentences

Name: _____

My Speaking and Listening Goal

I would like to improve on _____
_____
_____

To meet my goal, I will
1. _____
2. _____
3. _____

GOAL!

Start Date	Progress	Victory Date

START

Awesome   OK   Need Help

Name: _____

My Speaking and Listening Goal

I would like to improve on _____
_____
_____

To meet my goal, I will
1. _____
2. _____
3. _____

GOAL!

Start Date	Progress	Victory Date

START

Awesome   OK   Need Help

Name: _____   Date: _____

Speaking and Listening Self-Check

This discussion was about _____

_____

_____

_____

_____.

 Strengths

For this discussion, I

- O prepared ahead of time.
- O followed the rules.
- O carried out my role.

 **Goals for Next Time**

During this discussion, I

- O listened to others.
- O listened even if I disagreed with someone.
- O considered others' ideas.
- O looked at the speaker.
- O contributed to the discussion.
- O used evidence to support my points.
- O built on others' ideas.
- O responded to questions.
- O asked questions when I did not understand.
- O respectfully agreed or disagreed.
- O took turns.

Rate Your Participation

4

3

2

1

130

Presentation Skills

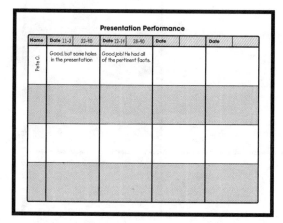

Use this form to track a student's progress with presentations throughout the year. Assess each student several times, such as quarterly. Complete the top of each column with the date and then a rating of your choosing, such as a rubric score or check marks. Use the section below to record any notes and observations, such as the topic of the presentation or strengths and goals.

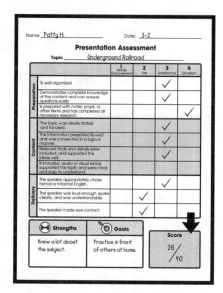

Use this page to record more detailed assessment information about a student's presentation. Mark an X in the appropriate column to rate the student's performance for each skill. If a skill was not covered, such as using visuals, mark through it. Use the *Strengths* and *Goals* sections to record observations about the presentation, or complete it when conferencing with the student after the presentation. Write the score out of the possible total and record it at the bottom right.

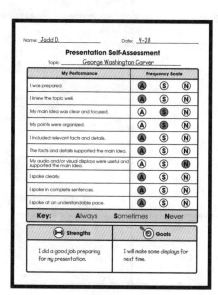

Provide students with copies of this page after their presentations so that they can assess their own performances. Have students record the topic of their presentations at the top. Ask them to assess themselves thoughtfully and circle the appropriate letter (key is below the chart) to rate themselves on each skill. Finally, have students record their strengths and their goals for their next presentations. You may choose to have students complete the bottom section during a conference about the presentation.

Presentation Performance

Name	Date				Date				Date				Date			

Name: _____   Date: _____

Presentation Assessment

Topic _____

		1 Needs Improvement	2 Fair	3 Satisfactory	4 Excellent
Preparation	Is well organized				
	Demonstrates complete knowledge of the content and can answer questions easily				
	Is prepared with notes, props, or other items and has completed all necessary research				
Content	The topic was clearly stated and focused.				
	The information presented flowed and was connected in a logical manner.				
	Relevant facts and details were included, and supported the ideas well.				
	If included, audio or visual extras supported the topic and were clear and easy to understand.				
Delivery	The speaker appropriately chose formal or informal English.				
	The speaker was loud enough, spoke clearly, and was understandable.				
	The speaker made eye contact.				

Strengths	Goals

Score

Name: _____   Date: _____

Presentation Self-Assessment

Topic _____

My Performance	Frequency Scale		
I was prepared.	(A)	(S)	(N)
I knew the topic well.	(A)	(S)	(N)
My main idea was clear and focused.	(A)	(S)	(N)
My points were organized.	(A)	(S)	(N)
I included relevant facts and details.	(A)	(S)	(N)
The facts and details supported the main idea.	(A)	(S)	(N)
My audio and/or visual displays were useful and supported the main idea.	(A)	(S)	(N)
I spoke clearly.	(A)	(S)	(N)
I spoke in complete sentences.	(A)	(S)	(N)
I spoke at an understandable pace.	(A)	(S)	(N)

Key: **A**lways   **S**ometimes   **N**ever

⊢⊣ Strengths	◎ Goals

Language Standards Crosswalk

Second Grade

Conventions of Standard English

- Use collective nouns; form and use common irregular plural nouns; use reflexive pronouns; form and use the past tense of common irregular verbs; use adjectives and adverbs appropriately.
- Produce, expand, and rearrange complete simple and compound sentences.
- Capitalize proper nouns; use commas in greetings and closings of letters; use apostrophes to form contractions and frequently occurring possessives.
- Use learned spelling patterns; consult reference materials to check and correct spellings.

Knowledge of Language

- Compare formal and informal uses of English.

Vocabulary Acquisition and Use

- Use sentence-level context as a clue to the meaning of a word or phrase.
- Determine meaning when a known prefix is added to a known word; use a known root word to determine an unknown word with the same root; use individual words to predict the meaning of compound words; use glossaries and dictionaries to determine meaning of new words.
- Identify real-world connections between words and their uses.
- Distinguish shades of meaning among related verbs and related adjectives.
- Use words and phrases acquired through conversations, reading, being read to, and responding to texts.

Fourth Grade

Conventions of Standard English

- Use relative pronouns and adverbs; form and use progressive verb tenses; use modal auxiliaries; order adjectives within sentences according to conventional patterns; form and use prepositional phrases.
- Produce complete sentences and correct fragments and run-on sentences.
- Correctly use frequently confused words.
- Use correct capitalization, punctuation, and spelling when writing.
- Use correct punctuation with quotations and dialogue; use a comma before a coordinating conjunction.
- Spell grade-appropriate words correctly, consulting references as needed.

Knowledge of Language

- Choose words and phrases to convey ideas precisely.
- Choose punctuation for effect.
- Choose when to use formal or informal language.

Vocabulary Acquisition and Use

- Determine or clarify the meanings of unknown and multiple-meaning words and phrases.
- Use context as a clue to the meaning of a word or phrase; use Greek and Latin prefixes, suffixes, and roots to understand unfamiliar words; consult reference materials.
- Understand figurative language, word relationships, and nuances in word meanings; understand simple similes and metaphors in context; recognize and explain common idioms, adages, and proverbs.
- Use antonyms and synonyms to better understand words.
- Learn and use academic and subject-specific vocabulary.

Language Concepts Checklist

Concept		Dates Taught			

Parts of Speech

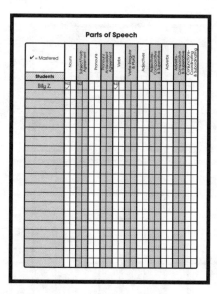

Use this sheet to keep track of the parts of speech you teach over time or in a unit. Record student names in the left-hand column. Six parts of speech and various subdivisions are listed. In the blank spaces below each, write the date you taught the concept in the left half. In the right half, use a marking system to indicate mastery. Then, you will have a record of when you taught the concept, who has mastered it, and who requires attention.

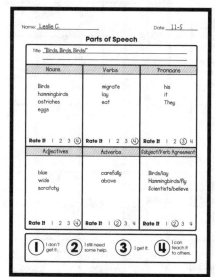

Use this versatile form to test understanding of any parts of speech or their subdivisions. Write the parts of speech you are studying above the six sections. Give each student a short text to read; either you or the student can record the title. During or after the reading, have students write examples of the parts of speech listed. Finally, have students rate themselves by circling the appropriate number in the rating scale. If you also want to rate students, use a different color of marker.

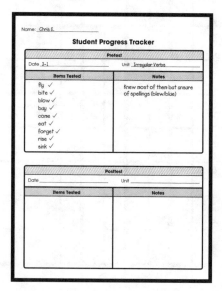

This form will help you track the material you have presented to individual students and whether they have mastered it. Write the date and the part(s) of speech presented. In the left section, list the items used to test students. Mark the items that students got correct or place a mark next to any errors. On the right, use the **Notes** section to record any observations or recommendations.

Parts of Speech

✔ = Mastered / Students	Nouns	Subject/Verb Agreement	Pronouns	Pronoun/ Antecedent Agreement	Verbs	Verbs–Irregular & Plural	Adjectives	Adjectives– Comparative & Superlative	Adverbs	Adverbs– Comparative & Superlative	Conjunctions– Coordinating & Subordinating

Name: _____   Date: _____

Parts of Speech

Title _____
_____

Rate It 1 2 3 4	**Rate It** 1 2 3 4	**Rate It** 1 2 3 4
Rate It 1 2 3 4	**Rate It** 1 2 3 4	**Rate It** 1 2 3 4

1 I don't get it. **2** I still need some help. **3** I get it. **4** I can teach it to others.

Name: _____

Student Progress Tracker

Pretest
Date _____   Unit _____

Items Tested	Notes

Posttest
Date _____   Unit _____

Items Tested	Notes

Simple, Compound, and Complex Sentences

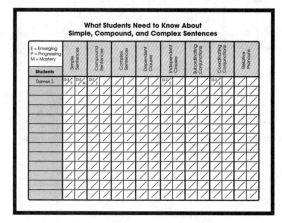

Use this form to teach simple and compound sentences. Students must be able to identify and write them. Students also need to learn about kinds of clauses, types of conjunctions, and relative pronouns. Teach coordinating skills, such as independent clauses and coordinating conjunctions when teaching compound sentences. This sheet will show who has mastered the concepts and who needs remediation. Write the date taught and *E*, *P*, or *M* to indicate mastery level. This form can also serve as a pretest and posttest record.

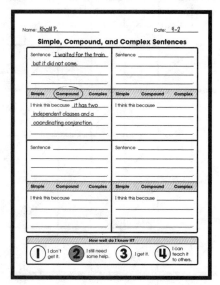

Use this sheet as a simple conference sheet or to allow students to show what they know about simple, compound, and complex sentences. Write sentences in the four boxes. Have students read each sentence, circle which kind of sentence it is, and give the reasons for their choice. (Note: If doing this with multiple students, write your sentences before photocopying.)

Use this form to allow students to show if they can distinguish between the three sentence types. You may also use the form as a posttest or used after you have presented one of the sentence types. Have students date the section they are working on and write an example sentence. Have students show that they know the sentence type by checking the appropriate boxes. This may send them back to fix a sentence that does not contain the requisite parts.

What Students Need to Know About
Simple, Compound, and Complex Sentences

Students	Simple Sentences		Compound Sentences		Complex Sentences		Dependent Clauses		Independent Clauses		Subordinating Conjunctions		Coordinating Conjunctions		Relative Pronouns	

E = Emerging
P = Progressing
M = Mastery

142

Name: _____   Date: _____

Simple, Compound, and Complex Sentences

Sentence _____

_____

_____

_____.

| Simple | Compound | Complex |

I think this because _____

_____

_____

_____.

Sentence _____

_____

_____

_____.

| Simple | Compound | Complex |

I think this because _____

_____

_____

_____.

Sentence _____

_____

_____

_____.

| Simple | Compound | Complex |

I think this because _____

_____

_____

_____.

Sentence _____

_____

_____

_____.

| Simple | Compound | Complex |

I think this because _____

_____

_____

_____.

How well do I know it?

1 I don't get it.   **2** I still need some help.   **3** I get it.   **4** I can teach it to others.

Name: _____

I Can Write a Variety of Sentence Types

I can write a simple sentence.   Date _____

_____

_____

_____

_____

I know this is a simple sentence because

○ it has a subject and a verb.

○ it expresses one complete thought.

I can write a compound sentence.   Date _____

_____

_____

_____

_____

I know this is a compound sentence because

○ it contains two independent clauses.

○ the clauses are connected with a coordinating conjunction.

I can write a complex sentence.   Date _____

_____

_____

_____

_____

I know this is a complex sentence because

○ it combines an independent clause with one or more dependent clauses.

○ it contains a subordinating conjunction or a relative pronoun.

Punctuation and Capitalization

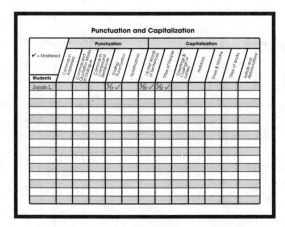

Use this page to record students' understanding of punctuation and capitalization concepts. Record students' names in the left column. Record the date you taught or assessed each concept at the top of the column, or you may choose to leave it blank if using informal assessments at different points in the year. Record the level of proficiency using a system of your choosing, such as check marks or an *E*, *P*, and *M* rating scale.

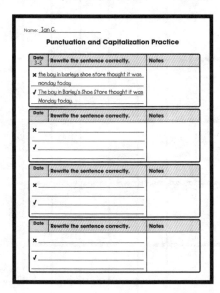

Use this page to assess individual students' success with punctuation and capitalization rules. Provide students with an incorrect sentence on the top line(s), and have them write a corrected version below it. (Note: If doing this with multiple students, write your sentences before photocopying.) Use the **Notes** section to record any observations. If desired, use this page as a one-time snapshot or once per quarter to create a portfolio of progress for the year.

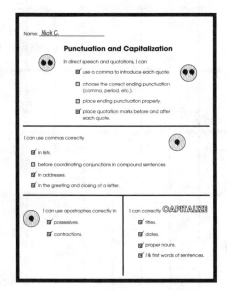

Provide students with this sheet to help them track and celebrate their understanding of correct punctuation and capitalization. As students master a skill, they should check off the appropriate box. If desired, have students add a date beside the description to record when they mastered the skill.

Punctuation and Capitalization

		Students												
Capitalization	Initials and Abbreviations														
	Titles of Works														
	Days & Months														
	Holidays														
	Greetings & Closings of Letters														
	Titles of people														
	I & First Words of Sentences														
Punctuation	Apostrophes														
	Ending Punctuation														
	Commas in Compound Sentences														
	Commas and Quotation Marks in Dialogue														
	Commas in Addresses														

✔ = Mastered

Name: _____

Punctuation and Capitalization Practice

Date	Rewrite the sentence correctly.	Notes
	✗ _____ _____ ✓ _____ _____	

Date	Rewrite the sentence correctly.	Notes
	✗ _____ _____ ✓ _____ _____	

Date	Rewrite the sentence correctly.	Notes
	✗ _____ _____ ✓ _____ _____	

Date	Rewrite the sentence correctly.	Notes
	✗ _____ _____ ✓ _____ _____	

Punctuation and Capitalization

 In direct speech and quotations, I can

☐ use a comma to introduce each quote.

☐ choose the correct ending punctuation (comma, period, etc.).

☐ place ending punctuation properly.

☐ place quotation marks before and after each quote.

I can use commas correctly

☐ in lists.

☐ before coordinating conjunctions in compound sentences.

☐ in addresses.

☐ in the greeting and closing of a letter.

 I can use apostrophes correctly in

☐ possessives.

☐ contractions.

I can correctly CAPITALIZE

☐ titles.

☐ dates.

☐ proper nouns.

☐ *I* & first words of sentences.

Vocabulary Acquisition

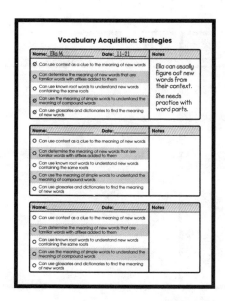

Use this form at any time to track students' progress as they grow as readers. You may use it in conference with individual students or with whole groups. The form will give you a quick look at students' abilities to use various strategies to learn new words. Keep these forms at hand so you can mark them any time you observe a student successfully using a particular strategy. Use the *Notes* section to record any observations.

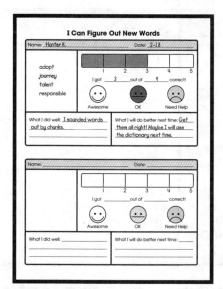

Use this form to allow students to show what they know of new vocabulary. Write up to five new words in the space on the top left. With or without context, allow students to use any of various strategies to figure out the meanings. After receiving feedback, have students date the form and rate themselves by coloring the bar and filling in a face to show how well they think they did. In addition, have students write about what they did well and what they will work on for next time. Use this form throughout the entire year.

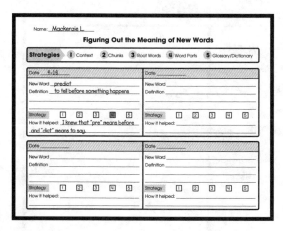

Students can more easily and quickly decode new vocabulary if they have command of various strategies. This form names five strategies, but you may add any others you prefer. After introducing these strategies, give students a short list of unfamiliar words. Allow students to decode the words using any of the listed strategies. Students will then write a word and its definition. Have students shade or color the number of the strategy that helped them and write how it helped.

Vocabulary Acquisition: Strategies

Name:_____ **Date:**_____ | **Notes**

○ Can use context as a clue to the meaning of new words

○ Can determine the meaning of new words that are familiar words with affixes added to them

○ Can use known root words to understand new words containing the same roots

○ Can use the meaning of simple words to understand the meaning of compound words

○ Can use glossaries and dictionaries to find the meaning of new words

---

Name:_____ **Date:**_____ | **Notes**

○ Can use context as a clue to the meaning of new words

○ Can determine the meaning of new words that are familiar words with affixes added to them

○ Can use known root words to understand new words containing the same roots

○ Can use the meaning of simple words to understand the meaning of compound words

○ Can use glossaries and dictionaries to find the meaning of new words

---

Name:_____ **Date:**_____ | **Notes**

○ Can use context as a clue to the meaning of new words

○ Can determine the meaning of new words that are familiar words with affixes added to them

○ Can use known root words to understand new words containing the same roots

○ Can use the meaning of simple words to understand the meaning of compound words

○ Can use glossaries and dictionaries to find the meaning of new words

I Can Figure Out New Words

Name: _____ Date: _____

1	2	3	4	5

I got _____ out of _____ correct!

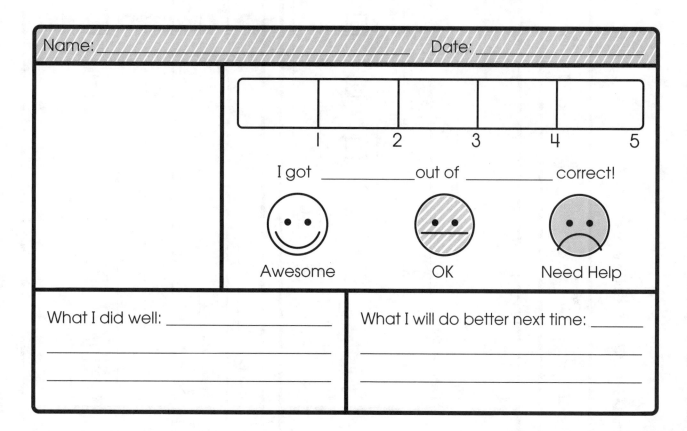

Awesome   OK   Need Help

What I did well: _____

_____

_____

What I will do better next time: _____

_____

_____

Name: _____ Date: _____

1	2	3	4	5

I got _____ out of _____ correct!

Awesome   OK   Need Help

What I did well: _____

_____

_____

What I will do better next time: _____

_____

_____

Name: _____

Figuring Out the Meaning of New Words

Strategies   **1** Context   **2** Chunks   **3** Root Words   **4** Word Parts   **5** Glossary/Dictionary

Date _____

New Word _____

Definition _____
_____

Strategy   ① ② ③ ④ ⑤

How it helped: _____
_____

Date _____

New Word _____

Definition _____
_____

Strategy   ① ② ③ ④ ⑤

How it helped: _____
_____

Date _____

New Word _____

Definition _____
_____

Strategy   ① ② ③ ④ ⑤

How it helped: _____
_____

Date _____

New Word _____

Definition _____
_____

Strategy   ① ② ③ ④ ⑤

How it helped: _____
_____

Prefixes, Suffixes, and Roots

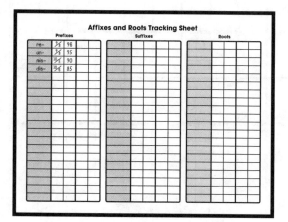

Use this page to track the affixes and root words taught throughout the year. Record the affix or root and the date taught to the right. After assessing class mastery, record the proficiency beside the date using a scale of your choosing, such as percentages, check marks, or *E, M, P*. If needed, reteach an affix or root and record the new date and level of proficiency.

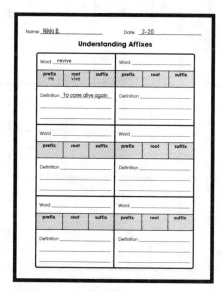

Assess students' individual knowledge of affixes and roots with this page. Present students with words that include prefixes, suffixes, or both written on index cards. Have students record a word in the top space, breaking it into its parts, and provide a definition. Be sure to include a mixture of affixes and roots to thoroughly assess students' understanding.

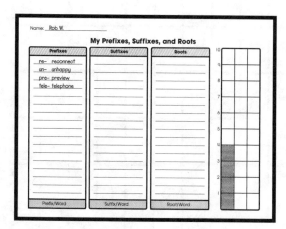

Provide this page to students to help them track the affixes and roots they have learned. As students prove mastery of an affix or root, allow them to record it in the correct section. Have them write both the affix or root and an example word. Periodically, students should count their lists and complete the bar graph on the right-hand side of the page, adding as necessary throughout the year.

Affixes and Roots Tracking Sheet

Roots

Suffixes

Prefixes

Understanding Affixes

Word _____

prefix	root	suffix

Definition _____

_____

_____

Word _____

prefix	root	suffix

Definition _____

_____

_____

Word _____

prefix	root	suffix

Definition _____

_____

_____

Word _____

prefix	root	suffix

Definition _____

_____

_____

Word _____

prefix	root	suffix

Definition _____

_____

_____

Word _____

prefix	root	suffix

Definition _____

_____

_____

Name: _____

My Prefixes, Suffixes, and Roots

	10	9	8	7	6	5	4	3	2	1

Roots

Root/Word

Suffixes

Suffix/Word

Prefixes

Prefix/Word

Figurative Language

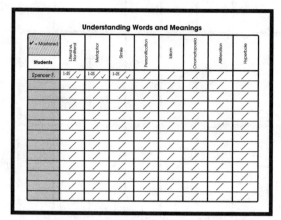

Use this sheet to track students' understanding of various types of figurative language. Record students' names in the left-hand column. As a student demonstrates proficiency with any skill, date and check the box. If you wish to use this sheet to record pretest and posttest data, keep dates and check marks on the left for pretest scores and the right for posttest scores.

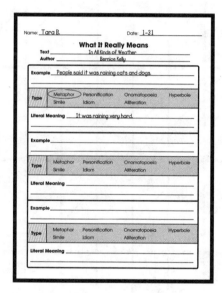

This form gives one student three opportunities to show what they know about the different types of figurative language. Send students on a scavenger hunt through a book or story to find sentences that contain examples of figurative language. Have students write the name of the book or text and author or source at the top of the page. Have students write an example sentence and then circle which type of figurative language it shows. Finally, have students write the literal meaning of the sentence or phrase.

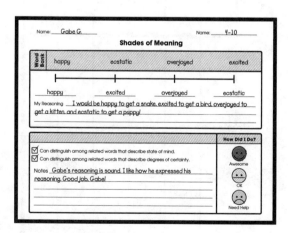

This form makes it easy to assess students' abilities to distinguish shades of meaning and the level of their reasoning skills. Give students four words that fit a category of state of mind or degree of certainty. Have students write the words in the *Word Bank* section and then place them in order from least to most. Then, have students write about the thinking behind the order they chose. There may be more than one acceptable answer, based on students' reasoning. Finally, make notes about your observations and allow students to rate their achievements.

Understanding Words and Meanings

Students / = Mastered	Literal vs. Nonliteral	Metaphor	Simile	Personification	Idiom	Onomatopoeia	Alliteration	Hyperbole

Name: _____   Date: _____

What It Really Means

Text _____

Author _____

Example _____

_____

Type	Metaphor Personification Onomatopoeia Hyperbole
	Simile Idiom Alliteration

Literal Meaning _____

_____

Example _____

_____

Type	Metaphor Personification Onomatopoeia Hyperbole
	Simile Idiom Alliteration

Literal Meaning _____

_____

Example _____

_____

Type	Metaphor Personification Onomatopoeia Hyperbole
	Simile Idiom Alliteration

Literal Meaning _____

_____

Name: _____

Date: _____

Shades of Meaning

Word Bank

My Reasoning _____

How Did I Do?

Awesome

OK

Need Help

☐ Can distinguish among related words that describe state of mind.

☐ Can distinguish among related words that describe degrees of certainty.

Notes _____